Bedford School's Secret Old Boys
and their Special Operations during World War Two

Bernard O'Connor

Bernard O'Connor's publications on or related to RAF Tempsford during World War Two:

RAF Tempsford: Churchill's MOST SECRET Airfield, Amberley Publishing, (2010)
The Women of RAF Tempsford: Heroines of Wartime Resistance, Amberley Publishing, (2011)
Churchill and Stalin's Secret Agents: Operation Pickaxe at RAF Tempsford, Fonthill Media, (2011)
The Tempsford Academy: Churchill and Roosevelt's Secret Airfield, Fonthill Media, (2012)
Agent Rose: The true Story of Eileen Nearne, Britain's Forgotten Wartime Heroine, Amberley Publishing, (2010)
Churchill's Angels: How Britain's Women Secret Agents Changed the Course of the Second World War, Amberley Publishing, (2012)
The Courier: Reminiscences of a Female Secret Agent in Wartime France, (Historical faction) www.lulu.com (2010)
Designer: The True Story of Jacqueline Nearne, www.lulu.com, (2011)
Return to Belgium, www.lulu.com (2012)
Return to Holland, www.lulu.com, (2012)
Bedford Spy School, www.lulu.com (2012)

Coming soon :
Churchill's School for Saboteurs: Brickendonbury, STS 17, Amberley Publishing, 2013

Purchase books online:
www.lulu.com/spotlight/coprolite

Visit Bernard O'Connor's website:
www.bernardoconnor.org.uk

Bedford School's Secret Old Boys

Contents:

Foreword

Introduction

Frank Nelson (1883 – 1966)

David Maitland Makgill Crighton (1914 – 1941)

Frederic 'Fritz' Peters (1889 – 1942)

Cecil 'Nobby' Clarke (1897 – 1961) and John Clarke

Harold 'Mike' Andrews (1897 – 1951)

Charles Bovill (1911 - 2001)

Bedford School's Secret Old Boys

Foreword

One of the wonderful things about being a Head Master, particularly of an institution with as rich a history as Bedford School, is to learn of, and to celebrate, the many achievements of alumni. Old Bedfordians (as we call them) do not disappoint; we have only to look at the trio of Paddy Ashdown, Al Murray and Alastair Cook, all of whom hit the headlines regularly. But as one ponders – with some pride – their achievements and exploits, one is drawn inexorably to the question 'what about the rest?' For education must surely be about more than those who go on to 'greatness'.

Of course, for those who are prepared to look, the information is there . . . hidden away perhaps but there nonetheless. And that is what is wonderful about this book of vignettes; what Bernard has done is painstakingly to search for detail to fill in the gaps, taking leads and pursuing them, building an overall picture, bringing individuals to life. And so we have six OB's resurrected, their stories told, their achievements noted.

As they should be. For there is something further about this little book. Bernard's passion and expertise in the area of special operations does much to lift the lid from some of the unheralded and murkier elements of war and espionage. And in these six stories, he has further enriched the priceless contributions boys from this school have made for their country. We only discovered a few years ago that Frederick Peters was the fifth OB awarded the Victoria Cross; we now know even more about him. And the other five we knew very little about at all. Now we do. And we honour their memories.

So, to appreciate the unsung heroes of the school; to simply to learn more about the exciting world of the SOE; to remember the contributions made in defence of freedom, read this book.

John Moule, Head Master of Bedford School

Bedford School's Secret Old Boys

Bedford School's Secret Old Boys

Introduction

In the 'Mem Hall' at Bedford School there are oak boards covering its walls with the names of 756 'Old Boys' who lost their lives during the First and Second World Wars. Some received honours for their actions and have had their stories told in newspaper articles, magazines and books. Most of these Old Boys, young men in their late-teens and early-twenties, have never had their stories told. A small number were involved in secret operations during World War Two and it is their stories that I have researched in an attempt to honour their memories.

On moving to the small village of Everton, about ten miles east of Bedford, I began researching the World War Two airfield that lies at the foot of the Greensand Ridge. Said to have been designed by an illusionist, RAF Tempsford was a top secret airfield from where, on the moonlit nights on either side of the full moon, pilots took off on missions to drop supplies to the various resistance groups in occupied Western Europe and to either parachute or land secret agents and bring back people to fight another day. The organisations responsible for arranging these missions and training the agents were initially the Secret Intelligence Service (SIS) and then the Special Operations Executive (SOE).

Having published a number of books on the airfield including *RAF Tempsford: Churchill's Most Secret Airfield; Women of RAF Tempsford; Churchill's Angels: How Britain's Women Agents Changed the Course of the Second World War; Agent Rose: The True Story of Eileen Nearne, Britain's Forgotten Wartime Heroine; Churchill's and Stalin's Secret Agents: Operation Pickaxe at Tempsford; Tempsford Academy: Churchill's and Roosevelt's Secret Airfield; Designer: The True Story of Jacqueline Nearne, a courier sent on a top secret mission to France during World War Two* and *The Courier*, a historical faction about a female agent sent into wartime France, I had learned how to ferret out information, built up a considerable library and developed useful contacts knowledgeable in the history of the Second World War.

When I joined the staff at Bedford School, I wondered whether any Old Boys had been involved in the Special Operations Executive. Contacting the archivist, to my surprise I found a few, so I researched their involvement and produced small booklets on them, which I deposited in the School library. Over the years, I have discovered more and felt that I should combine their fascinating stories into a book.

I need to acknowledge the assistance of Gina Elsby and Brenda Roberts for their help in locating snippets in the Old Boys' Archive; Lesley Harrison for her assistance in the Library; Niall Creed for his links to Bletchley Park; Ann Clark for help with her husband and father-in-law, Simon Andrews, Philippe Connart, Geoffrey Cowling, Adrian Finch, Scott Goodall, Leyre Solano Echeverria, Rog Stanton and Graham Ward and the British Embassy in Lisbon for details about Harold Andrews; Sam McBride for his research into Frederic Peters; Klas Nilsson for his work on Charles Bovill: Stephen Bunker for the research he did for *Spy Capital of Britain* and Steven Kippax for his comprehensive knowledge of the Special Operations Executive. I also need to thank the staff at the National Archives in Kew for providing me with access to several personnel and other files and the staff at Bedford, Sandy and Potton libraries for providing in and out of county books. Karoline Jeffery helped with the front page design.

It is to the memory of the following Old Boys that this book is dedicated: Harold Andrews, Charles Bovill, John Vandepeer Clarke and his father Cecil 'Nobby' Clarke, David Maitland Makgill Crighton, Frank Nelson and Frederick Peters.

Bedford School's Secret Old Boys

Frank Nelson (1883 – 1966)
Bedford School OB (1893-1897)

Born on 5th August 1883 in Bentham, Gloucestershire, Frank Nelson started what until the 1920s was called Bedford Grammar School when he was eleven. His father, the general manager of the Army and Navy Auxiliary Co-Operative Supply, like many men working for the British military and Colonial Office, took advantage of the relatively cheap Harpur Trust schools to educate his son. When he died, Frank and his mother, Mrs Catherine Nelson, lived firstly at 53 Bromham Road, and then later at 23 Conduit Road in Bedford. (Bedford School, OB Archives; Oxford Dictionary of National Biography)

In 1897, when he was 14, Frank left Bedford and, according to his obituary in The Times, went to Germany to study at Neuenheim College, Heidelberg. After leaving College, he travelled to Bombay, India, as an assistant with Symons, Barlow and Company, rising to become a senior partner.

During the First World War he joined with the Bombay Light Horse but was seconded to work in intelligence duties. There was no permanent Intelligence Corps at that time, most officers were seconded from their original Regiment or Corps. No record of what he actually did has come to light. In 1922, when he was 39, he was made chairman of the Bombay Chamber of Commerce, and the following year was made President of the Associated Chambers of Commerce of India and Ceylon.

Acknowledging his contribution to the British Empire, he was knighted in 1924 when he was 41. Returning to Britain, he was elected Conservative Member of Parliament for Stroud in Gloucestershire in the May 1924 election. Later that year, a number of Conservative MPs with a wartime intelligence background played an equivocal role during the 'Zinoviev Letter 'controversy. Published in the Daily Mail, it purported to be from the Communist International in

Moscow encouraging the Communist Party in Great Britain to intensify industrial unrest. Acknowledged later as a forgery by MI6, Britain's Secret Intelligence Service (SIS), its publication led to the downfall of Ramsay MacDonald's Labour government. According to his Who's Who entry, he led a four-MP delegation to Russia in 1926 and was part of a Parliamentary group visiting Australia in 1927.

Nelson was re-elected in 1929 but the economic depression forced him to resign his seat in May 1931 so that he could concentrate on his business interests. For a number of years he was the joint managing director of Lamson Paragon Supply Company in London which manufactured cash ball carrying technology for the retail industry. (The Times Obituary August 13th, 1966)

Shortly after the Second World War started in 1939, he was appointed as the British Consul in Basle, Switzerland. Exactly what his work entailed has not come to light but no doubt he used his political, diplomatic and international business experience to further British interests. Michael Foot, the military historian, quotes him having had experience of Secret Service work whilst in Basle and knew about security and intelligence. Most sources identify him as being one of about 200 members of the 'Z' Organisation. This was an independent intelligence-gathering network run by Claude Dansey, the assistant head of SIS and directed from Bush House on the Strand. (http://intelligenceref.blogspot.com/2010/11/z-organisation.html; Foot, M.R.D. (1999), SOE: The Special Operations Executive 1940 – 1946, Pimlico, p.23; Stafford, D. (1980), Britain and European Resistance 1940 -1945, Macmillan, p.36; Martin, D. SOE - An Amateur Outfit?; Andrew, C. Secret Service, Jeffrey, K. (2011), MI6, Bloomsbury Publishing)

William MacKenzie's classified wartime report on the Special Operations Executive (SOE) makes reference to 'C', the codename for Sir Stewart Menzies, the head of

Bedford School's Secret Old Boys

Sir Frank Nelson (1893-1897) , first head of the Special Operations Executive during World War Two.
(http://www.specialforcesroh.com/gallery.php?
do=gallery_image&id=2351&gal=gallery&type=full)

SIS, appointing Nelson as a replacement for Major Lawrence Grand, the head of its Section D. The D was said to stand for Destruction. Nelson's business background probably reflects the original SOE focus on economic sabotage rather than the work it is later famous for. Part of the section in Mackenzie's account dealing with Nelson's appointment was redacted (removed) on National Security grounds. (MacKenzie, S. (2002), The Secret History of S.O.E: Special Operations Executive 1940-1945, St Ermin's Press; Author's communication with Niall Creed)

By the summer of 1940, Nelson must have impressed Lord Dalton, the Minister of Economic Warfare (MEW), who had been entrusted by Winston Churchill with the task of establishing the SOE, as he was appointed its first head in mid-August 1940 with the codename 'CD'. SOE was created by combining SIS's Section 'D' (Destruction), MI (R), (Military Intelligence Research) and EH (Electra House) and entrusted by Churchill "to set Europe ablaze". According to the Special Forces Club website, Section 'D', under Major Lawrence Grand,

> *had been developing plans and resources for undermining Germany's economy and war potential by such unconventional means as sabotage, subversion and propaganda, but which had begun to get out of control since Grand's imagination and enthusiasm were not matched by his management ability; MI(R), a 'think-tank' of the Military Intelligence Directorate of the War Office, led by Major J.C.F. ('Joe') Holland, another Royal Engineer whose staff, among many other initiatives, had made a deep study of the doctrine and methods of guerrilla warfare and had developed the first Special Forces training school at Inverailort in Scotland; and Electra House (EH), the secret propaganda arm of the Foreign Office, formed by Sir Campbell Stuart after the Munich crisis.* (http://www.sfclub.org/history.htm)

Bedford School's Secret Old Boys

With the support of Sir Stewart Menzies, Sir Alexander Cadogan, the Head of the Foreign Office, and the Heads of the Armed Forces, Dalton divided SOE into three branches: SO1 for underground propaganda, SO2 for unacknowledgeable operations, sabotage, and supporting the resistance groups in enemy-occupied countries, and SO3 for planning. Nelson was initially appointed head of SO2 but then assumed responsibility for SO3 when it merged in January 1941 and had overall responsibility for SOE after SO1 was taken over by the Political Warfare Executive in August 1942.

He had oversight of most of SOE's early operations, assisted by Gladwyn Jebb, Assistant Under-Secretary of the Ministry of Economic Warfare, and Robin Brook, who was responsible for recruiting and controlling secret agents. (Foot, op.cit. p.23)

In order to have a military rank so that he could exercise his quasi-military functions, he joined the RAF Voluntary Reserve as a pilot officer. According to Who's Who, he was commissioned in 1940 and appointed Acting Air Commodore the following year. It has been suggested that it was the RAF rather than the Army or Royal Navy because the RAF did not have quite as strenuous age restrictions. (Author's communication with Niall Creed)

Every day, he held meetings at 9 o'clock at SOE's headquarters at 64 Baker Street to which he summoned all those who had important business to discuss. To assist SOE's operations, the Royal Air Force created two Special Duties Squadrons who, until early 1942, used the racecourse at Newmarket. When RAF Tempsford, a top secret airfield, about ten miles northeast of Bedford School, was completed, they were based there. Designed to give overflying enemy pilots the impression it was a disused airfield, it only operated after dark on the nights on either side of the full moon. 138 Squadron was responsible for dropping supplies to the resistance movements in occupied Europe and parachuting in secret agents. 161 Squadron was responsible for landing and pickup operations on remote fields, navigating only by the light of the moon.

Bickham Sweet-Escott, one of SOE's regional directors who worked for a time as Nelson's personal assistant, described him as having had,

> ... a formidable task. Not only was there not a single agent in enemy-occupied France, but SOE was a new body for which no precedent existed. As such it incurred the suspicion and jealousy of the established secret organisations of the Foreign Office and the service ministries, all of which were professional bodies which had existed for many years and which were concerned by the inevitable amateurishness at first displayed by SOE. Another difficulty was recruitment, for by the autumn of 1940 most men of ability were employed elsewhere. Above all Nelson found he had to obtain for SOE facilities, such as secret wireless sets, aircraft for parachute training and getting agents into Europe, and special devices for sabotage. But it was no easy task to get these scarce resources unless SOE could show results, and without the resources there could be no results. Finally, he had somehow to gain the confidence of Whitehall and the services. (Sweet-Escott, B. (1965), *Baker Street Irregular*. Methuen, London)

Nelson set to work at once with tireless energy, and surrounded himself with a group of able people, notably Colin Gubbins, who at first took charge of the important job of training and operations and was to finish the war as head of SOE. Gradually Nelson overcame the difficulties by his unshakeable integrity of purpose. It was a disappointment to him when in early 1941 the chiefs of staff ruled against supplying secret armies in Europe by air in favour of the bombing offensive. (www.oxforddnb.com/view/article/35198)

What helped change attitudes towards the SOE were two

Bedford School's Secret Old Boys

carefully planned operations. In Freddie Clark's Agents by Moonlight, he detailed how, at midnight 14/15th March 1941, Flight Officer Oettle took off from Tempsford and dropped Captain Berge, four other agents from Charles de Gaulle's Republique Française Section and two canisters of small arms at Morbihan, east of Vannes in Brittany. They landed 5 miles (8 km) from the intended drop zone. Their operation, codenamed SAVANNA, was to disrupt the German bomber 'pathfinder' squadrons based at Meucon airfield. This very high quality trained unit had been responsible for the raids on Coventry and other cities. Submarine crews from Brest and Lorient were also stationed at the base. The plan was to ambush the bus carrying the crews out on leave to Vannes and kill all on board. When the agents made further enquiries they discovered that the bus was no longer running, the troops arrived in twos and threes by car. Although the op was aborted, Berge dispersed his team to reconnoitre the surrounding countryside and sound out the local population about their willingness to participate in anti-German activities on behalf of General de Gaulle. However, when Berge and three other team members were 'lifted out' by the pilot of a small Lysander plane, they brought back with them a mass of intelligence about living conditions, curfew times, local rules, restrictions, identity papers, ration cards, railway timetables, prices of cigarettes and other everyday items – all invaluable to the SOE instructors.

On 10th April 1941, Oettle flew six Polish saboteurs to destroy the electric transformer station at Pessac in Bordeaux. It was providing power for the German submarine base at Bordeaux. Anything that could be done to reduce the impact the Germans were having in the Battle of the Atlantic would be welcomed. An electrical fault over the Loire released their containers miles from the intended DZ so the pilot returned to base. The plane crashed on landing injuring the whole party. A second attempt was made on the night of 11th/12th May. Group Captain Hockey and

Squadron Leader Jackson flew a Whitley to Bordeaux on operation JOSEPHINE. Three RF agents, Captain A. Forman, R. P. Calard and Lt. Varnier were said in the official report to have been parachuted in blind, with no reception committee, but Berge, their Captain, stated they dropped near Mimizan to a committee he'd set up earlier. On reconnoitring the transformer station they couldn't get past the guards, the 9 ft (2.7 m) wall and the high-tension wire. When they failed to make contact with the submarine which attempted to pick them up on the 20th May, they contacted the agent who'd been left behind from the first mission.

Not to be outdone they lay low for a month, used specialist gear to get past the security fence, climb the wall, open the main gate and set their explosive and incendiary charges. Six of the eight transformers were blown up. The charges slipped off the other two before exploding and the party escaped. The disruption to the Bordeaux area took the Germans several months to recover from. The supply to the submarine base was affected, as well as to local factories supplying war materials for the Germans and the electric railway over much of southwest France. 250 people were reported as arrested, the Pessac area was fined 1,000,000 French Francs and twelve German sentries were shot. The four agents eventually returned to Britain after many adventures. Dalton contacted Churchill about the success of the mission.

We may therefore take it as practically certain that three trained men, dropped from one aeroplane, have succeeded in destroying an important industrial target. This strongly suggests that many industrial targets, especially if they cover only a very small area, are more effectively attacked by SOE methods than by air bombardment... I hope that with the cooperation of the RAF we shall be able to repeat this form of attack during the coming autumn and winter. (Clark, F. (1999), *Agents by Moonlight,* Tempus Publishing)

As a result more aircraft were allocated to the Special Duties Squadrons to enable similar operations elsewhere.

By the winter of 1941, SOE was in touch with agents and supporters in most of the countries of occupied Europe. Above all, Nelson made people believe that, given facilities, results could be achieved. In less than two years SOE had become an established force with the confidence of the chiefs of staff, and was recognised in every theatre of war. It is no disparagement of his successors to say that he created the groundwork without which SOE's later successes in Europe and the Far East would have been impossible.

According to the Stroud History website,

With his past experience as a Member of Parliament and in international commerce he was well qualified for the task. Although never very strong physically he threw himself into his new task with all he had to give and it needed everything. The establishment of a new and secret department, responsible to no existing department and with a charter of almost limitless scope, naturally aroused hostility, veiled or open throughout the length and breadth of Whitehall. That he was able before his retirement through ill-health in the spring of 1942 largely to overcome this inherent animosity and to get his organisation accepted and recognised as an essential development in modern warfare was due entirely to his force of character, his patent honesty of purpose and complete unselfishness. He wore himself out in the process but left a solid base on which his successor could build. Frank Nelson was a man of grim but unshakable determination, with a strong sense of loyalty and of organisation. (http://www.stroud

-history.org.uk/articles. php?article_id=11)

During his term in office, he oversaw SOE and SIS operations as far north as Norway, east as far as Poland and south as far as North Africa. Notable missions undertaken whilst he was in charge include Operation ANTHROPOID, the dropping of Czech agents whose mission was to assassinate Reinhard Heydrich in Prague and Operation GROUSE, the attack on the heavy water plant at Vemork, Norway. (Clark, F. (1999), *Agents by Moonlight*, Tempus) His major achievement, according to Foot, was

> *To convince sensible heads of departments that SOE existed, was not to be shrugged off, had to be taken seriously, and was working against the common enemy, axis tyranny. While he did so, Nelson had also to insist that SOE was a secret service, so word did not spread far down the hierarchy. Lesser bureaucrats could not abide a body that was secret, powerful, and outside their control.* (Foot, op.cit.pp.29-30)

When he retired due to 'ill-health', his role as head of the SOE was taken over by Charles Hambro, his deputy, who at thirty had been the youngest ever director of the Bank of England. After recuperating he had a brief spell working at RAF's Intelligence Headquarters in Whitehall. In May 1942, Nelson was created Knight Commander of St Michael and St George. He then served as a Wing Commander in Air Intelligence on the British Staff in Washington and finished his war service as an Air Commodore, commanding the Air Intelligence Section in the Control Commission in Germany. (*Who Was Who, 1960-1971*) He died on Thursday, 11 August 1966 in Oxford at the age of 83. (*The Times*, Obituary, 13 August, 1966)

Bedford School's Secret Old Boys

David Maitland Makgill Crighton
Bedford School (1925 – 1933)

David Maitland Makgill Crighton was born 13 July 1914 in Poona, India, into a military family, the third child of Lieutenant Colonel David Edward Maitland Makgill Crighton, who was commissioned as a Queen's Own Cameron Highlander and remained one all his life. His mother, Phyllis, nee Cuthbert, returned to England with the children and settled in Hereford, where Edward was born on 23 November 1916.

Of all the Old Bedfordians who worked in the SOE, it was David who got the most coverage in the Ousel. Research by Gina Warboys of the Old Bedfordians Club has revealed that he started at Bedford School with his brother Edward, 'Jock', on 15 January 1925 and left at the end of the Summer term 1933. Over his eight years at the school, he was a monitor, Head of Bromham, in his House XV, sub-editor of the Ousel, Secretary of the Debating Society and Editor of Mosaic, a poetry magazine. He had reached Lance Corporal in the Officers' Training Corps by January 1933.

There are various entries for him in the Ousel. David and Edward played tennis as a pair in doubles and entered the Hayward Wells Racquets and reached the fourth round in 1933. David received the F R Hockliffe Memorial English prize for prose in 1931. He played for his house in the house rugby matches in 1932 and both David and Edward played together in the senior house teams in 1933. There are reports of a number of debates that David took part in - one being the proposition 'That in the opinion of this House, Lending Libraries benefit neither authors nor readers' in 1931. Another in 1932 was 'This house considers Home Rule to be the only practical solution of the Indian Problem' when he gave his opinion that 'as the Indians were entitled to Home Rule, it was a question of whether they were yet prepared for it. We would be failing in our duty if we did not aid that preparation; but if we were furthering it, then the motion was justified'.

Bedford School's Secret Old Boys

David was then the proposer for the next debate on which the Ousel reported:

The second meeting of the term was held on Sunday, February 21st, when the motion before the house was that "This house views with regret the tendency of the Cinema to usurp the position of the Theatre." 'Mr. D.M.M. Crichton [sic], no doubt speaking with elaborate preparation, bade fair to give us a thorough presentation of the case for the theatre. He complained that if the Cinema was art, it was mechanised art, inferior to the Theatre as expressing life, lacking continuity, and, in spite of appearances, unrealistic. Continuing to exploit a facility in epigram, Mr. Crichton declared that the Cinema's gain in scope was its loss in artificiality. The Theatre was representative of life and the Cinema representative only of the Theatre. This masterly display of logical antithesis nearly awed us into believing that Mr. Crichton had supported the motion. We were expecting just a little substance, when Mr. Innes, complete with Film Weeklies,- Quarterlies, Monthlies, etc., not to mention biographies of Lubitsch and Marlene Dietrich, took his cue, and we knew the game was on. For Mr. Innes was equally airy, equally plausible, we nearly wrote, equally logical. But Mr. Innes seems unable to escape from the wooliness of his political doctrines.' The debate was carried 46 votes for the motion against 33 against.'

He also features greatly in debates in the Ousels in 1933 when he was Secretary of the Society – he opposed the motion 'Team spirit is more valuable than individual enterprise and it is written,

'Mr. Crichton was elusively lucid. Like the proverbial Assyrian he descended upon Mr. Brown, who, *exhausted probably by his own meanders, was unfortunately asleep. But it takes, however, more than a sleeping beauty to disturb the Secretary, and, quite unperturbed, he kept the noiseless tenor of his way. Destroying small pieces of papyri at an alarming rate, he made the house ring with his eloquence for the next five minutes. Though quite irrelevant, the Secretary concluded by offering his usual thanksgiving to the Deity that he was not a Conservative.'*

There are other reports in the Ousel of other debates and he also spoke in the Alchemists discussion on Scientific Method in Feb 1933. David also wrote an editorial for the Mosaic in 1933 and appeared in the 'Election Impressions' in the Ousel literary Supplement in 1931 and wrote a full piece on 'The Death of Shelly' in the same edition. One of his poems was published in Mosaic:

Night (In the Modern Style)
By D. M.-M.-CRICHTON.

DAYLIGHT has fled :
Dark is the bleeding sky :
Engines go screaming by
Into the dead.
Everywhere night
Over all substances
And in the distances
Drives away light.
Somewhere an owl on high
Hoots to the hollow sky
Moonily bright.
Storm clouds are flying and babies are crying and bishops are dying
To-night.

Bedford School's Secret Old Boys

Jupiter rises, stars at his side ;
Over the heavens the windy clouds ride,
The waves on the beaches are beating.
Trees on the hill-tops mutter and sigh :
Harry and Minnie (they're lovers) steal by
Where day into darkness was fleeting.
Somewhere an owl on high
Hoots to the hollow sky
Moonily bright.
Storm clouds are flying and babies are crying and bishops are dying
To-night.

Light will come ; light will come
Out of the east and over the grey :
Darkness will vanish and sadly uncover
To the eyes of watchers
The fields where she lay.
Go to sleep Gabriel,
Turn over Vyvyan,
Close your eyes Antony,
Soon comes the Day
Over all substances
And in the distances,
Bringing light with the shaving-water
And boats to the bay.

On leaving Bedford School, he read Modern History at Worcester College, Oxford and there is a report in the Ousel after he had left that: *'D.M.M. Crichton, lately a Sub-Editor of the Ousel and Editor of Mosaic, has been appointed fourth Editor of the Isis at Oxford. He hopes this time next year to be Editor-in-Chief. His rapid rise to journalistic fame is attributed to his association with the Ousel of Bedford School, a journal which, so it appears, carries much weight in Oxford literary circles.'* Another Old

Boy at Oxford wrote in the Ousel in 1933 that:

'Crichton lost no time in entering into the life of the University —he spoke at the Union on more than one occasion. By half-term he was appointed to the Editorial Staff of the Isis (the undergraduate weekly) ; whether it was on account of his literary ability or his triple-barrelled name (he is known as Maitland-Makgill -Crichton now) I do not known. Crichton is now up all night, either at sherry parties or writing, cutting, setting or performing similar duties pertaining to one in such an exalted position.'

Whilst at Oxford, David was already veering into politics where he ultimately saw his future. In 1935 he edited 'Tory Oxford', a small collection of essays written by several like-minded students. His contribution was 'The Menace of Fascism.'

Details of his life after graduating with a 3rd class degree are sparse. He worked as a free-lance journalist in the late-1930s, which funded his travelling. He spent many months in Albania, where, amongst other things, he researched the life of King Zog. On returning to Scotland, he decided to enter politics and was the prospective Scottish Unionist candidate in his family homeland of West Fife. However, when war broke out, he followed his family tradition and joined the army, rising to the rank of Second Lieutenant in the Royal Northumberland Fusiliers.

However, his knowledge and experience of living overseas brought him to the attention of the Foreign Office which was keen to recruit people with an understanding of the political situation in south-eastern Europe. It was Kenneth Mason, David's Oxford University professor, who put his name forward to M.I.R (Military Intelligence Research). (TNA HS9 372/1)

Given the strategic importance of the Balkans (Serbia

and Albania), David's work on King Zog was considered valuable. On 30 November 1940, he was contacted by M.O.9. (Military Operations) S.O.2, SOE's sabotage section and asked to attend an interview in Room 055A, a small, bare room in the basement of the War Office in Whitehall, London. This was MI5's 'front office', where potential recruits to the nation's internal counter-intelligence and security agency were vetted.

Records of his interview are to be found in his personnel file in the Special Operations Executive section of the National Archives in Kew. On 6 March 1940, he completed a form describing himself as single, Church of England, good at tennis and golf and still playing games. He gave his address as 32 Albion Street, London, W,2, telephone number Paddington 6744. In response to the question: special Knowledge: a) Propaganda, he wrote: 'Yes, both politically and abroad for Journalism.' He was twenty-five, five feet ten inches tall, had fair hair, blue eyes and was 'a good, vigorous type with contacts, particularly in Albania.' (TNA HS9 372/1)

Four days later, he was interviewed by Lt. Col. J.S.A. Pearson, codenamed D/HV. All the personnel in the intelligence services used codenames in letters, telegrams and memoranda to prevent their identities becoming known to the enemy. Pearson then sent a memorandum of the interview to Colonel G. F. Taylor, codename A.D., who was the director of SOE's overseas groups:

Colonel [Edmund de Renzy-] Martin and 2nd Lieut. David Maitland MacGill [sic] Crighton
I interviewed today at the War Office Maitland Makgill Crighton, who you will remember, was writing a life of Zog and who produced a memorandum which circulated through the Foreign Office, the War Office and here.
He claims a certain friendship with Zog, and was in Albania for a year, chiefly I gather getting material for

Bedford School's Secret Old Boys

The 1,522 tons SS Jonathan Holt, which was sunk on 24 February 1941 by a German submarine off Fastnet with the loss of David Maitland Makgill Crighton on his way to Egypt on an SOE mission

(http://discoveringbristol.org.uk/images/sized/images/uploads/slavery/ Photograph12-400x303.jpg; http://www.jhplc.com/images/body-jhcl-01.jpg)

his book and at the same time doing a certain amount of free-lance journalism. He is young and I imagine intelligent, and certainly keen. I might add that he was at the outbreak of war standing as prospective unionist candidate, for West Fife.

I suggest that it would be of value to have an unofficial contact with Zog here in London, and that this contact should be Col. Martin, who as you know is at present in the Spanish section. An immediate decision on this point should be taken, and if it is agreed that Maitland Makgill Crighton with the ultimate object that Zog should go out to Greece or Albania, he should have near him not only an Englishman he knows and trusts, but also men who are in close contact with us and can interpret our views to him whenever desirable.

The only value of Maitland Macgill Crichton, as far as I can see it, would be if he really is friendly with Zog and if that friendship is reciprocated. I think we could get a check on this if Martin was allowed to sound Kastrati, Zog's secretary, in order to find out their feelings towards Crichton. If he is acceptable he is the only man we have heard of yet who could travel with Zog and act as general A.D.C. [Aide-de-Camp] *to him.* (TNA HS9 372/1, 3 December 1940)

Almost a month later, after the start of a new year, Pearson wrote to D/Army:

This officer called here this morning and we put up to him the proposal that having been asked for by Colonel [Dayrell R.] Oakley-Hill at Belgrade, he should proceed there as soon as possible.

He is prepared to go and the next step is to get his release from the army as soon as we possibly can.

As soon as his release goes through he can come to this office and learn the latest position in Albania prior to his departure.

We hope this will go through fairly quickly.
His regiment is Royal Northumberland Fusiliers, and present address, HQ, Northumbria Area, Darlington. (Ibid, 2 January 1941)

He signed the Official Secrets Act on 27 January 1941 and the following day, his transfer from his regiment was approved. There is no mention in his file of him attending the SOE's assessment course, going on paramilitary training in northwest Scotland, doing parachute training at Ringway aerodrome or attending their 'Finishing School' at Beaulieu in the New Forest for a course on clandestine warfare.

The SOE had a politically sensitive mission planned for him which would have entailed detailed briefing sessions. On 18 February someone in SOE's office in 64 Baker Street, codenamed D/H.19, wrote a memorandum to Lieutenant Colonel E. E. Calthorpe, codenamed D/T1, the Head of SOE's Security Section.

David Maitland Makgill Crighton
Personnel number P/121526
The above agent is leaving London tonight for Liverpool. He is proceeding to Cairo by a convoy scheduled to leave Liverpool tomorrow. He is proceeding to Takoradi and Cairo for the Balkans.
His passport is No. 363043 issued by the Foreign Office 18th February 1941 and he is described as a Civil Servant. Will you please make the necessary arrangements with the Security Officer at Liverpool to facilitate his passage through Customs etc. Ceases to be specially employed and is entitled to pay and allowances from Army Funds. (Ibid. 18 February 1941)

David embarked on the 1,522 tons SS Jonathan Holt, a British Cargo Steamer, on a roundabout route to Egypt via

Sierra Leone. However, the ship was attacked by a German U-boat off Fastnet, 61'10N 11'55W on 24 February and sunk. He was lost, presumed drowned. (http://www.specialforcesroh.com/ roll-4066.html) It was not until a month later that the SOE informed his mother.

Room 237
It is with the deepest regret that I have to inform you that your son, 2nd Lieutenant D. Maitland Makgill Crichton, has almost certainly lost his life at sea owing to enemy action.

From all evidence available, there are only three survivors from the ship in which he was travelling, and it seems conclusive that no-one else was saved.

Your son was serving at the time in a post for which his very high qualifications had particularly suited him; and his loss if one which this country can ill afford.

Will you please accept this expression of my very deep sympathy in your loss. (TNA HS9 372/1 27 March 1941)

It may be of interest to note that David's cousin, Diana Rowden, who was living in France before the war, escaped over the Pyrenees and got back to Britain in 1941. Recruited by the SOE, she was trained as a courier and parachuted into the Jura, southeast France but was caught and executed in the Natzweiler concentration camp. Her story can be found in 'Churchill's Angels: *How Britain's Women Secret Agents Changed the Course of the Second World War*'.

Bedford School's Secret Old Boys

Frederic 'Fritz' Peters (1889 – 1942)
Bedford School OB 1900 – 1901

Frederic Peters was born on 17 September 1889 in Charlottetown, Prince Edward Island, north-eastern Canada, the son of the Attorney General and the first Liberal Premier of the island. His family nicknamed him 'Fritz' because of his obsession with all things military, probably encouraged by his grandfather who had been a soldier. After moving to Victoria in British Columbia and later Esquimault, he developed a fascination with the sea. Visiting naval bases with his father and watching British warships passing by his home which overlooked the Salish Sea, that inspired him to join the Navy.

In 1900 his parents moved to Bedford, England, where his mother had relatives. For a time they lived at 52 de Parys Avenue and later at 15 Oaklands Road. Frederic and one of his brothers attended Bedford School and his elder sister Mary went to Bedford High School for Girls. Frederic was only was at Bedford for a year as his parents sent him in September 1901 to Cordwalles School, in Canterbury, where they had naval classes.

Returning to Canada, when he was sixteen he joined the Royal Nay in Esquinault, British Columbia in 1905 and attended Naval College. In 1912, when the HMS Titanic was sunk, he was a twenty-two-year-old lieutenant serving in the Royal Navy's China Station at Weihaiwei on China's north-eastern coast. Retiring in 1913, he worked as third engineer with the Canadian Pacific Railways ships that plied the interior of British Columbia.

When the First World War broke out he re-joined the navy as lieutenant second-in-command of the destroyer HMS Meteor and was involved in several sea battles. When the ship's engine room was hit by shells from the German cruiser Blucher in January 1915 during the Battle of Dogger Bank, he rescued two ratings, bravery for which he was 'Mentioned in Despatches' and was the first

Canadian to be awarded the Distinguished Service Order. In 1918 he won the Distinguished Service Cross for 'showing exceptional initiative, ability and zeal in submarine hunting operations and complete disregard of danger, exceptional coolness and ingenuity in his attacks on enemy submarines." With enemy submarines being a constant threat, his navy colleagues particularly admired his courage and skill in hazardous sea rescues. His letters to his family show that he hated self-promotion and publicity, kept a low profile and was extremely modest about the medals he received, preferring not to wear them unless ordered to. (Email communication with Sam McBride, his great nephew, 31 May 2012)

His brother John 'Jack' Peters, a Bedford School Old Boy (1900 – 1903) died during a German gas attack on the 7th British Columbian battalion in Ypres on 24 April 1915. His other brother Gerald, fighting in the same battalion was killed in the Mount Sorrel counterattack in the Ypres Salient on 3 June 1916.

Retiring with the rank of Lieutenant Commander, Frederic spent most of the inter-war years in the Gold Coast, what is now Ghana, manufacturing specialised pumps for midget submarines. He re-joined the Navy in 1939 and commanded a flotilla of anti-submarine trawlers and heading a naval intelligence staff section. Sinking two German submarines in the North Sea, earned him a bar to his Distinguished Service Cross. To be then chosen to be the Commandant of an industrial sabotage school, must have been a big change after years at sea.

It may well have been his experience in sinking ships and submarines that attracted him to the attention of the British Secret Intelligence Service. After war broke out in 1939 a sabotage section was established, known as D Section. One of its members, Guy Burgess, later discovered to have been a Soviet 'mole', suggested that the SIS ought to have a special sabotage school, which he suggested should be named 'Guy Fawkes College.'

Bedford School's Secret Old Boys

11-year-old Frederic 'Fritz' Peters at Bedford School in 1901
(Courtesy of Sam McBride)

Bedford School's Secret Old Boys

Laurence Grand, the head of D Section, agreed and he was allocated Brickendonbury Manor, a secluded mansion in its own extensive grounds, outside Hertford, about twenty miles north of London. Kim Philby, a Cambridge University friend of Burgess and another Soviet mole, was given the task of drawing up an outline of what was needed to be taught and Frederic was given responsibility for the school's administration.

Sam McBride, Frederic's great-nephew, told me that his great-uncle was very involved in plastic explosives and time delay fuses, the wherewithal the 'students' were practising with on their course. Philby recalled an amusing incident that occurred before Frederic left to take up other work.

Night had just fallen after a fine summer day. The Commandant was in bed, nursing a sharp attack of eczema, to hide which he was growing a beard. A visiting instructor under the name of Hazlitt, was at his bedside sipping a glass of port. There was a sudden shout from the garden, which was taken up by a Babel in five languages. Trainees poured into the house, claiming to have seen, one, three, ten, any number of parachutes falling in the vicinity. On hearing the news, the Commander ordered the Belgians to get into uniform and mount a machine-gun in the French-windows. It commanded a nice field of fire, right across the school playing grounds. I do not know what would have happened if the enemy had come in by front door. "If the Germans had invaded," the Commander told Hazlitt, "I shall get up."

He then made a disastrous mistake. He instructed Guy to ascertain the exact facts of the case, and telephone the result to the duty officer in London. Guy went about the business with a wicked conscientiousness. I heard snatches of his

Bedford School's Secret Old Boys

Frederic Peters circa 1918.
(Courtesy of Sam McBride)

subsequent telephone report. "No, I cannot add to what I have said. ... You wouldn't want me to falsify evidence, would you?" Shall I repeat? ... Parachutes have been seen dropping in the neighbourhood of Hertford in numbers varying from eighty to none ... No I cannot differentiate between the credibility of the various witnesses. Eighty to none. Have you got that? I will call you again if necessary. Goodbye." He went to report in triumph. I don't know what I shall do if I do get up," said the Commander, "but I shall certainly take command."

An hour or two passed, and nothing happened. The Belgians sadly took apart their Lewis gun, and we all went to bed. Next morning, Guy spent a lot of time on the telephone, and periodically spread gleeful tidings. The Duty Officer had alerted his Chief, who had communicated with the War Office Eastern Command had been pulled out of bed, its armour grinding to action stations in the small hours. Guy made several happy guesses at the cost of the operation, upping it by leaps and bounds throughout the day. I should add that the nil estimate given him the night before was my own; the eighty, I should think, came from Guy himself. Both of us were wrong. One parachute had fallen. Attached to a land-mine, it had draped itself harmlessly round a tree. (Philby, K. *My Secret War: The Autobiography of a Spy*, Arrow Books, 2003, pp.20-22)

Philby claimed that Frederic had grown increasingly taciturn and withdrawn over the summer of 1940. Word spread that Section D was to be absorbed within the newly formed SOE under the control of Dr Dalton, the Minister of Economic Warfare. Grand's place was taken by Frank Nelson, another Bedford School Old Boy, who was described by Philby as 'a humourless businessman'. This was shortly followed by a visit to Brickendonbury by Colin Gubbins, Nelson's second-in-command,

'Fritz' Peters, RN, Commanding Officer of Brickendonbury Manor, Hertford, (STS 17), Industrial Sabotage School c.1940
(Courtesy of Sam McBride)

'and a posse of fresh-faced officers, who barked at each other and at us, the Commander fell into a deep depression. He minded not being told. It was no surprise when he summoned Guy and myself one morning and told us that he had spent the previous evening composing his letter of resignation. He spoke sadly, as if conscious of failure and neglect. Then he cheered up and the charming smile came back, for the first time in many days. He was clearly happy to be going back to his little ships after his brief baptism of political fire. (Philby, op.cit. p.22-23)

After the SOE took over the running of the school, Frederic returned to the Navy and was given command of HMS Tynwald, an anti-aircraft cruiser in the Far East. He returned to England in August 1941 to assume duties as a Special Operations and naval planner in Operation Torch, the Allied invasion of North Africa. In this capacity, he advised Winston Churchill, the then Prime Minister, and the Admirals of the British and American navies.

His replacement at Brickendonbury was Cecil Clarke, known as 'Nobby'. He had been involved with the early development of the limpet bomb in his workshop on Tavistock Street in Bedford. His son John, who was at Bedford School between 1938 and 1946, helped him test them in Bedford Modern swimming pool. Their story is told later. In John's account of his war years, he mentioned his father being involved in the planning for Operation Reservist, part of Operation Torch, in which Peters played a part. This was an attempt to make an early morning landing of Allied troops in Oran harbour in Algeria, about 280 miles east of Gibraltar, surprise the Vichy French and capture their ships and port facilities to prevent them from falling into German hands. The rest of the Torch operation involved subduing the coastal defences of North Africa, improving Allied positions in the Western Desert and defeat Hitler's Afrika Korps.

A. S. Field's 1943 impression of the attack on Oran harbour, Algeria, led by Frederic Peters on 8 November 1942.
http://www.nationalarchives.gov.uk/theartofwar/img/pics/works/INF3_0472.jpg

According to McBride, Frederic had a sabotage specialist on board his ship. In fact, he had more. In Mark Reardon's article, Death at the Hands of Friends: Oran, he mentions twelve British Special Boat Service operatives having six 'folbots', folding kayaks, and 'mobile mines' to destroy the inner and outer boom protecting the entrance to the harbour. One presumes they were trained by Clarke in their use at Brickendonbury. Three teams under the command of Captain Harold Holden-White went on the HMS Walney. The other three, under the command of Lieutenant E. J. Lunn, went on the Hartland. (Reardon, M. J. Death at the Hands of Friends: Oran, Army History, Winter 2011, p.16, 18; Edwards, Seven Sailors, Collins, London, 1945, pp.232-3)

Flying American flags in the hope that the French would not attack, in the early hours of 8 November 1942, Frederic commanded the 250-foot destroyer HMS Walney and accompanied by the HMS Hartland, two boats carrying British Commandos, soldiers of the 6th US Armed Infantry Division and a small detachment of US Marines. The saboteurs were not needed as he succeeded in ramming through the double boom of logs, chains and coal barges and sailed the one and a half miles towards the jetty. It was not the surprise they expected. Spotted by searchlights, they came under constant fire from four onshore batteries, a light cruiser, and several anchored destroyers.

Despite releasing smoke screens, both ships suffered numerous direct hits. Frederic was the only officer on the bridge to survive but was wounded in the shoulder and blinded in one eye. His ship, on fire and disabled, reached the jetty before sinking with flying colours. He and thirteen surviving crew members made it to the shore and were arrested. The other ship, HMS Hartland, was blown up and sunk with the loss of half its crew. Of the 393 Allied troops on board the two ships, 183 died and 157 were wounded, including 113 dead from the Royal Navy and 86 wounded, five US Navy dead and seven wounded. (Atkinson, R. An Army at Dawn, Holt Paperbacks, New York, 2002; Reardon, M. J. Death at the Hands of Friends: Oran, Army History, Winter 2011, p.16)

All the survivors were captured and imprisoned but, two days later, they were all freed when the French garrison surrendered to the Americans. By that time the French had systematically destroyed the harbour facilities, meaning that his operation had failed but the other Allied landings at Casablanca and Algiers succeeded. The London Gazette reported on 18 May 1943 that, 'On being liberated from the gaol, he [Frederic] was carried through the streets where the citizens hailed him with flowers.' In recognition of his bravery of what was called 'a suicide charge', Dwight D. Eisenhower awarded him the Distinguished Service Cross, a U.S. decoration second only to the Medal of Honour. Their citation stated that:

Captain Peters distinguished himself by extraordinary heroism against an armed enemy during the attack on that post. He remained on the bridge in command of his ship in spite of the fact that the protective armor thereon had been blown away by enemy shell fire and was thereby exposed personally to the withering cross fire from shore defenses. He accomplished the berthing of his ship, then went to the forward deck and assisted by one officer secured the forward mooring lines. He then with utter disregard of his own personal safety went to the quarter-deck and assisted in securing the aft mooring lines so that the troops on board could disembark. At that time the engine room was in flames and very shortly thereafter exploded and the ship turned on its side and sank." (In McBride, S. *The Bravest Canadian,* Granville Publishing (2012))

Research by McBride, detailed how, on 13 November 1942, three days after his release, he was flown back to

England in a Sunderland seaplane, which encountered lightning, hail, sleet and forty-knot headwinds and then dense fog as it approached Plymouth Sound. Instrument failure resulted in the plane hitting the water, flipping over and splitting apart about a mile and a half from the entrance to the Devonport Dockyard near Plymouth. Miraculously, the eleven Canadian crew members survived. The four other passengers were killed in the crash or died from exposure in the water but Flight Lieutenant Wynton Thorpe, the pilot, found Frederic still alive 'and valiantly tried to drag him to safety as he swam to a breakwater, giving up in exhaustion after about an hour when it was obvious that Peters was dead. A rescue boat from shore arrived about half an hour later to pick up survivors.' (Sam McBride's article on the Naval and Military museum's website)

    The British government posthumously awarded Frederic the Victoria Cross. With no known grave, presumably his body sank in Plymouth Sound, he is commemorated on the Portsmouth Naval Memorial and Mount Peters, near Nelson in British Columbia, was named in his memory in 1946.

Bedford School's Secret Old Boys

Cecil Vandepeer Clarke 1897 – 1961
Father of John Vandepeer Clarke, Bedford School OB

In a list detailing the locations used by Office of Strategic Services, the United States' intelligence agency set up during the Second World War, I noticed 'Area K Bedford, Special Operations – Demolition School'. Intrigued, I tried to locate where exactly in Bedford it was, who was involved and what role it played during the war. I contacted The Bedfordshire and Luton Archive Service and Lydia Saul, Keeper of Social History, at the Cecil Higgins Gallery Bedford Museum. I was told about the reminiscences of John Clarke, one of Bedford School's Old Boys. Ann Hagen at Bedford Museum had transcribed them for the BBC's WW2 People's War website. They revealed that his father, Cecil Vandepeer Clarke, had a property on Tavistock Street in Bedford that the Americans called 'Area K'. On contacting John's wife, Anne, she very kindly supplied me with photographs and other documents about her father-in-law's secret war work and gave me permission to include them in this work.

Born on 15 February 1897, Cecil Vandepeer Clarke grew up in London and was known to his friends as Nobby. He attended Greenwich Hospital School and the Grocers' Company School but when the First World War broke out in 1914, he abandoned his studies at the University of London for a two year certificate course with the Officer Training Corps. After getting an 'A' in the Combined Training Course, in 1915 he was gazetted as a Second Lieutenant in the Devonshire Regiment. Transferred to the Ninth Battalion South Staffordshire Regiment, 23rd Division, he served as a Captain in the British Expeditionary Force in France. In October 1917 he was sent to Italy where he was awarded the Military Cross for taking part in the decisive battle of Vittorio Veneto. During that time he served as an

41

Officer in a Pioneer Battalion which involved doing a great deal of tunnelling and general explosives work. In fact, he was said to have loved making loud bangs.

After the Armistice was signed in 1919, he moved to Bedford and became director of the motor manufacturing firm, H.P. Webb and Co. Ltd. In 1924 he bought 172-3 Tavistock Street, a residential property with an adjacent commercial garage and started his own motor engineering firm. (TNA HS 9/321.8)

In his spare time he built his own four cylinder motor car engine in the workshop behind the premises. However, his new product did not make money as the major car manufacturers of the time could produce similar engines more cheaply. He realised that there was a space in the market for trailers of one kind or another. Most two-wheeled trailers were unstable when pulled behind a vehicle, so he designed them with a low-slung chassis, close coupled wheels and a special suspension system. Accordingly, he set up his own business, LoLode (Low Loading Trailer Company), which specialised in manufacturing low loading trailers that could be towed behind vehicles.

'Nobby' married Dorothy Aileen in August 1928 and they had three children, John, David and Roger. His eldest son dictated his reminiscences of his childhood in pre-war Bedford to Ann Hagen of Bedford Museum. Whilst some are long, they are worth including as they are a first-hand account of wartime Bedford, life at school and the top secret work his father was involved with.

As a child John attended Froebel Teaching College School in The Crescent under the guidance of a Miss Spence. From there he went to Bedford School. In an interview with the Bedford Museum for the BBC's World War Two People's War, he told how,

> *We used to trot along the 200 or 300 yards to the very friendly atmosphere of the school. I stayed there until I was nine or ten when I passed the entrance exam to go*

Bedford School's Secret Old Boys

Cecil 'Nobby' Clarke, MC, (1897 – 1961), limpet bomb developer, Explosives Expert, Commanding Officer at Brickendonbury Manor 1940-42
(Courtesy of Mrs John Clarke)

to Bedford School in the Preparatory Department.

Before the war Bedford was a much smaller town, it was only about 40,000 population and we had a very quiet life. There was a regular pattern of school, and holidays were generally spent in the town but every summer we would have a fortnight's holiday away, generally in South Wales. My father and mother would take us off to The Gower for a wonderful time on the beach and on the cliffs there in South Wales.

When I'd finished at the Training College School and went to Bedford School, this was in 1938 at the time of the Munich Crisis. By which time my father was getting very concerned as an ex-Army Officer from the First World War when he had won the M.C. (Military Cross) for his work in Italy and France; he was getting very concerned that the country was heading for another war with Germany. He started making preparations for what might happen and I remember trenches being dug and Air Raid Precautions starting and I believe he was the ARP [Air Raid Precaution] Officer for Bedford, for the period immediately before the war.

I used to go again on foot up Tavistock Street. It must be the most familiar street to me from my memories of Bedford, full of shops some of which haven't changed at all since that time. Up to the corner of De Parys Avenue and initially to the Preparatory Department, the Prep School known as the Inky at Bedford School where I was for two years. I was in the top class and I did fairly well. We were taught in the first year by a very pleasant young exchange teacher from Canada whose name was Mr. P. A. Bridle and he was known actually to us children as 'Pa'. He got us in the first year into the rudiments of school life at Bedford School and left

Bedford School's Secret Old Boys

'Nobby' Clarke demonstrating his prototype limpet mine at his home in Tavistock Street, Bedford c.1939
(Courtesy of Mrs John Clarke)

after a year. He was in fact lucky to survive his return journey which had started before the war. But as he was on the liner Athenia, he had the unlucky distinction of being one of the first people to be sunk by a German U boat only a day or two after the commencement of war in 1939. [On 3 September 1939, over 100 lost their lives.]

I remember September the 3rd, 1939 very clearly standing to attention in our house while the National Anthem was played and hearing [Neville] Chamberlain [the then Prime Minister] speaking. We had help in the house because my mother was the Company Secretary of the Low Loading Trailer Company; therefore we had a maid and we had a cook as well. We could hear they were in tears in the kitchen as they heard the news. Then a few minutes later the air raid sirens sounded but it was a false alarm. It sounded over London and I think for good measure they thought they'd better include Bedford, just in case German planes came over. (http://www.bbc.co.uk/ww2peopleswar/stories/34/a5961134.shtml)

By 1937, Clarke had designed the chassis for a 'double-decker' caravan and had a local Bedford company make the coachworks. It had a built-in toilet and separate shower with hot and cold running water. He claimed that passengers could sit in the main saloon and pour out drinks without spilling them.

Despite of the economic and political problems during the late 1930s, he ensured that his family had a chance to get away from it all. John recalled how

We went on holiday with our lovely caravan which by that time, because myself and my younger brother, three years younger than me, were getting larger and larger. My father decided to take the unusual step of having the original 1937 caravan with its wonderful lines somewhat spoiled. It was but not too bad looking

Bedford School's Secret Old Boys

Brickendonbury Manor, SIS and then SOE's Industrial Sabotage outside Hertford where 'Fritz' Peters and then 'Nobby' Clarke were commanding Officers 1939 – 1942
(Courtesy of www.brickendonbury.co.uk and Neil Rees)

but very unusual looking, providing a second storey on the caravan. So we had a double-decker caravan with room for the boys, that's myself and my brother, to sleep in the upstairs accommodation which we reached by a ladder coming down off the back of the caravan, out of doors. I distinctly remember in 1939 we went on holiday after all the experimentation on the limpet mine had been completed; we went to North Wales and we had to be very careful because there were a great number of low bridges. Every time, as we left Bedford, we would stop if there was a low railway bridge and approach very cautiously to see whether we'd got the inch or two clearance we needed to get through without taking the caravan top off. But after a while I must say my father, temperamentally he got rather blasé about this and just charged at every bridge he came to - fortunately without any real damage to the caravan. I remember going through North Wales, standing, which I'm sure would be contrary to Health and Safety Regulations today, on the catwalk on the roof of the original caravan outside of our cabin and getting a fine view of the countryside as we went along the A5 through North Wales. Then we came back and the war started. (http://www.bbc.co.uk/ww2peopleswar/stories/34/a5961134.shtml)

Life at Bedford School during World War Two was very different for John. In his reminiscences he recalled how,

...we had a much more Spartan regime I think than before the war. But it was only gradually introduced because, for example, important things like the Tuck Shop where you could buy sweets and chocolate at the School was well stocked up in the first few months at the beginning of the war. So it was only gradually

Bedford School's Secret Old Boys

Limpet mines being carried by 'student' at the Industrial Sabotage School, Brickendonbury Manor, c.1942

(Courtesy of Mrs John Clarke)

Bedford School's Secret Old Boys

that the pain of deprivation from familiar things like bananas and oranges and so on really hit home. But quite apart from that, life was extremely disciplined at Bedford School in those days. We were a public school with a long tradition, founded in 1552, and everybody was very carefully monitored and looked after but it was a very busy school regime. We would start as usual as most schools at about 9 o'clock in the morning. I was a 'day boy' and I should say that 30-40% of the boys at the school were in boarding houses grouped around the School Campus. I was one of the 'day boys' at the school and my brothers subsequently went to Bedford School. The typical school day would be arriving at school just before 9 o'clock, two hours in the morning period, then break for 20 minutes. This was not an uncontrolled sort of break but was very disciplined in that we were marched out by Forms and were taken by senior boys who were either Monitors or Options, in other words, Prefects, either senior or junior in status, to do physical exercises. PE, very vigorously for about a quarter of an hour which left us about five minutes to chat with friends and then back to work for the second half of the morning session. Then we had prayers and having had Morning Assembly first of all we would have brief prayers at 1 o'clock and then go home. If we were living close enough, we could go home for our lunch and be back within the hour. In the afternoons we had on Mondays, Wednesdays and Fridays we had further school lessons until about 4 o'clock.

But on Tuesdays, Thursdays and Saturdays, these were Games days. And the usual sort of regime with rugger in the winter months, rowing in the winter months and in the summer too and cricket in the summer with a whole host of minor sports which

Bedford School's Secret Old Boys

Demonstration of Clarke's 'Tree Spigot' being fixed to a tree at Brickendonbury c.1942

(Courtesy of Mrs John Clarke)

everyone was supposed to enjoy and many people did. I particularly enjoyed playing 'Fives' but apart from that there were things like gymnastics, boxing and so on as extra curriculum things. You were expected to do your ordinary games and then in addition to that you were normally expected to take part in some secondary sport. So sport was a very important part of the Bedford School experience.

We also, as I got further up the school, we found ourselves in the JTC, that's the Junior Training Corp which was originally, in the First World War, had been called the Officer Training Corps and then it was the Junior Training Corps and later on I believe it was given another name CCF – (Combined Cadet Force). We were in the JTC and then I found an opportunity to escape from the JTC which meant that we had in the JTC Regular Army training under the auspices of Sergeant Majors who were on the school staff. I found that I was able, during the latter part of the war, to transfer to the ATC, the Air Training Corps which was slightly less military and more interesting because we had the occasional opportunity of having a flight in the Royal Air Force planes at nearby aerodromes either at Henlow or Cranfield. I enjoyed a couple of very nice trips in Avro bi-planes. As one of the perks of belonging to the ATC we were supposed to know all about aeroplanes and identification and so on; I don't think any of us got terribly good at it but it was preferable to being in khaki. One thing I was very pleased that I did not have to do in the ATC was to participate in the wrong part of a group which went out to Cranfield. We were split up for flight experience. We were split into two groups, this was probably 1945, and half of us went up in a perfectly innocuous bi-plane and I was allocated as part of that group. I was very pleased I was on that side because the others were invited to, or told, to take their places in

Bedford School's Secret Old Boys

Demonstration of Clarke's 'Plate Spigot' at Brickendonbury
c.1942

(Courtesy of Mrs John Clarke)

Bedford School's Secret Old Boys

a glider and we watched the glider being towed up. That was alright but when it came down we were astonished to see the glider, detached of course from the towing aircraft, coming down at an angle of about 45° degrees at great speed until it was about 20 feet above the ground, it suddenly flattened out and it landed. I'm afraid that my friends who had drawn the wrong ticket came out looking extremely green! Laughter! As a result I was very pleased that I had not had to participate in glider training. I think this was a normal landing technique. They gathered enough speed to come down at the right angle. Anyway we watched horror stricken as this thing came down. We thought all our friends had had it. A view that was much more intensely felt by those on the glider!

Our holidays in the war years were necessarily not the same sort of pattern as before the war. We had to spend time in Bedfordshire primarily. We had School Camps as I got into the upper part of the school and we had a very enjoyable time harvesting one summer (about 1942 or 1943) in Stewartby at the Brick Works. In their model village at Stewartby they had a few spare empty houses and we were accommodated there and well fed in the London Brick Works canteen. These were all very new buildings at that time because the estate was only built in the 1930s. We were taken out on trucks to help bring in the harvest, stooking and so on in the nearby farms which were in fact in the ownership of the Brick Company which had valuable resources of clay for brick making underneath them. At that time the London Brick Company had no need or intention to obtain. They had acquired a whole series of farms in this clay bearing area so that for future development they could get their clay for making bricks. I well remember our lunches were uniformly bread and dripping [beef fat] throughout the three weeks I think of our time in harvesting. (http://

Bedford School's Secret Old Boys

www.bbc.co.uk/ ww2peopleswar/stories/52/
a5961152.shtml)

When Clarke submitted an advertisement for inclusion in the journal Caravan & Trailer, it brought him to the attention of its editor, Stuart Macrae, who also edited the 'Science Armchair' magazine. Macrae visited Clarke's workshop to inspect the caravan and, in Winston Churchill's Toyshop, his memoirs about his war years, described him as *'a very large man with rather hesitant speech, who at first struck me as being amiable but not outstandingly bright. The second part of the impression did not last long.'* (Macrae, S. (1971), *Winston Churchill's Toyshop*.p.8)

He subsequently wrote what was described as a very favourable article about the caravan which must have generated some trade and forged a link between the two men. In June 1939 Macrae was entrusted by the War Office's M.I.R.c. (Military Intelligence Research) section with the task of producing a magnetic device that could be attached to the hull of a ship and explode after a time delay, Impressed at the way Clarke dealt with problems in an unorthodox way, he decided that he might be able to help.

Although I had not seen him since this initial visit, Clarke's unusual personality and his ability to view mechanical problems in an unorthodox way had always stuck in my mind. I decided that he was the man for me, jumped into my motorcar complete with rough drawings and my collection of magnets, and went off to Bedford. I had of course rung up Clarke to warn him that I was coming and given him a very guarded idea of what I wanted to talk about. He was operating from his private house which he had converted in some remarkable way into a works. Sweeping a number of children out of his living room which had also to serve as an office, he filled me with bread and jam and some awful buns and then we got down to business. Nobby, as I soon came to call him, was enthusiastic as I knew he would be. 'Fine! How about starting tomorrow? Be here as early as you can. Stay here if you like; we can easily find you a bed.' (Macrae, S. (1971), *Winston Churchill's Toyshop*.p.8)

This link extended throughout the Second World War and involved top secret work for Winston Churchill and the Special Operations Executive. The scientists and technicians who were involved in the design and manufacture of top secret weaponry were called 'boffins' or 'backroom boys'.

To assist him in his project, Clarke used the outbuildings behind the family home as an experimental workshop. John recalled his father often being in the workshop during the first months of the war, working on a limpet mine, a top secret new weapon with enormous potential for the war effort. John went on to state that,

When, in 1939, Macrae was asked by somebody in the War Office if he could assist with the procurement or getting information where such things could be procured, whether he could supply or find a supplier for limpets and he was not told initially what they were for. But after his security clearance had been established with the War Office, Macrae was told that the idea was to provide limpet mines that could sink enemy shipping. So he said, 'I will do my best to design something with a colleague of mine whom I know and the two of us together, I think we can produce something for the use of British Forces.' (Ibid.)

He'd got a short time but as he said, he'd got 'a bag of gold' from the War Office to do everything that was necessary. He contacted my father and came down to Bedford and the two got on very well - they'd known

Bedford School's Secret Old Boys

each other before because of the caravan experience. They cleared all the children out of the room where they were discussing the matter and then started to get the design together. It was very much an ad hoc way of approaching the thing but both were brilliant at lateral thinking and the two men within about a month (this was in June/July 1939) before the war, had evolved a practicable Mark I type of limpet mine.

As the eldest boy, I was then 10 years old, I took a keen interest in what was going on and I knew broadly speaking what this was about. I was told not to say anything about it to my schoolboy friends. But the interesting thing about the limpet mine was that it was very much Bedford home-made. The two men visited Woolworths and they got washing up bowls made of spun aluminium to contain the explosives. (http://www.bbc.co.uk/ww2peopleswar/stories/34/a5961134.shtml)

Macrae recalled them cajoling a local tinsmith into stopping all the other work he was doing and fashion some rims with annular grooves to fit the bowls and plates they had bought. These were then screwed in place to allow the rims to close.

The rims were sweated to the bowls and as many of the little horseshoe magnets as possible were packed into the annular grooves so that the pole pieces were exposed, these pole pieces then being lined up by simply placing a keeper ring over the whole lot. To secure the magnets in place we at first poured bitumen into the groove, but later found that plaster of Paris was a better answer.

The idea was to stuff this bowl full of blasting gelatin or some similar high explosive and then screw the lid in place so that the device was sealed. It had to be carried by a swimmer, so we contrived a belt consisting of a 4" wide steel plate, just long enough to span the magnet ring, to which were attached strips of webbing which could be tied round the swimmer's waist. Obviously the swimmer must not be unduly handicapped by having to travel under water with this contrivance so we wanted it to weigh next to nothing when submerged. Eventually, after using up all the porridge in the house in place of high explosive for filling, juggling about with weights and dimensions, and flooding Nobby's bathroom on several occasions, we got this right. (http://www.bbc.co.uk/ww2peopleswar/stories/34/a5961134.shtml)

After testing it in his bath, the field trials took place in Bedford Baths, which belonged to Bedford Modern School at the top of Clarendon Street, only about 200 yards away from the Clarke's household. Given the nature of their experiments, the baths were closed to the public during these tests. A large steel plate was propped up against the wall of the deep end to represent the side of a ship. Macrae appreciated Clarke being an excellent swimmer.

Looking as if he were suffering from advanced pregnancy he would swim to and fro removing the device from his belt, turning it over, and plonking it on the target plate with great skill. We learned a lot more than when we had been in the bathroom. Our magnets were so powerful that when in the water it at first proved difficult to remove the mine from the keeper plate belt without the risk of rupturing oneself. So we had to experiment with various sizes of plate until we had one which gave the required hold and no more. The buoyancy too came in for adjustment as we found it advantageous to have slight positive buoyancy. (Macrae, op.cit.p.9)

John was often taken along to watch, and presumably enjoy swimming in an otherwise empty pool. He recalled how,

A swimmer would be loaded up with the limpet mines before swimming to the side of a ship and plant the charge against the side using magnets on the underside of the limpet mine. Hence the curved shape with the magnets underneath it looked like a gigantic limpet when it was attached to the hull of a ship. My father gallantly undertook all these tests himself with a steel plate strapped around his tummy and the charge on the limpet mine attached to it. He had quite a lot of problems with adjusting the number of magnets to be used. If it was too strong you just couldn't get the thing off and were struggling underwater with a very heavy metal casing on your tummy.

... There they were, swimming up and down and plonking them on a steel plate at the deep end and this worked well. Then to simulate the effect of a ship having had a limpet mine planted on it, all unsuspected, deciding to get underway and move through the water we had to ensure that the drag of the water on the limpet mine on the side of the hull wouldn't cause it to come away.

I remember going with my father in the motor boat and we trundled up and down the Ouse at different speeds with this underwater device, which nobody could see because it was under the water. And we demonstrated that the launch could travel up to 10 or 15 knots and the limpet mine was still firmly attached. So that was yet another test that my father had to undergo and it was all extremely interesting and exciting. I would repeat that this was done just before the war started. (http://www.bbc.co.uk/ww2peopleswar/ stories/34/a5961134.shtml)

The next trials were done on the River Ouse. In Alan Crawley's research into Clarke's work he stated that 'A steel plate was attached to the side of a motor boat and a limpet mine was held against it below the water line. They then went up and down the river at different speeds to find the strength of magnet that was required to hold it to a ship's hull in motion.' (Crawley, A. 'The Limpet Mine & 171-175 Tavistock Street', *BAALHS*, April 2012) John Clarke was allowed to travel in the boat and remembered being very excited by it all.

Back at the workshop, Macrae christened their new magnetic device 'The Limpet'. What they hoped was that the enemy kept their ships in good condition as it wouldn't stick to a hull covered in barnacles.

The next problem they had to solve was the 'delayed action initiator'. Various types had to be devised which would detonate the limpet after a delay of anywhere between half an hour and two hours after it was stuck on the ship. As there was nothing on the market at that time, they needed

> *... a spring loaded striker, maintained in the cocked position by a pellet soluble in water. When the pellet dissolved, the striker would be released to hit a cap to initiate a detonator which would explode a primer to explode the main charge. All this was easy enough, but finding a suitable pellet was difficult. There were too many variables. The powder itself was the first one, and the degree to which it was compressed the second one. The temperature of the water made all the difference, and of course so did whether it was fresh water or sea water. Expert chemists were called in to find us the answer, but they failed. One day a pellet would dissolve at a rate that alarmed us and would no doubt have alarmed a Limpeteer. The next day, a similar one might take several hours over the job and we did not want that. There was some hope of a Limpet staying put on a stationary target and every chance of its getting washed off if the target moved off at 20 knots or so as it might well do in time.*
>
> *One of Nobby's children solved the problem for us. It was only a small one and, in sweeping it off the bench which it much preferred to its play pen, we upset it by*

> *knocking its bag of aniseed balls on to the floor. Whilst Nobby was doing the consoling act, I tried one of these sweets. It seemed to stay with me a long time, getting smaller and smaller with great regularity. After trying a couple himself Nobby agreed that this might well be the answer so we commandeered the remainder of the supply and started to experiment. I think I can safely claim to be the first man to drill holes into aniseed balls and devise a fitting to enable this to be done accurately and efficiently. We rigged up some of our igniters with these aniseed balls in place of soluble pellets, and the next day the children of Bedford had to go without their aniseed balls.* (Macrae, op.cit.p.9)

It must have been quite exciting for John as he recalled having to visit all the sweet shops in Bedford and purchasing all their supplies of aniseed balls. Michael Simmonds, John's friend who lived opposite on Clarendon Street, recalled playing with him in his garden.

> *One day, I remember, he took us into his father's factory/workshop. We were very interested, of course, and wondered why there was someone, a lady, I think, drilling holes in aniseed balls. We were told that these were for making necklaces for children to suck in hospital! We believed this and were given the crumbs from the drillings to eat. Sweet rations were short, so we were glad of a little extra! Little did we know then that the aniseed balls were really for fuses for limpet mines to be attached to enemy shipping! When the aniseed ball dissolved in the sea water, it activated the bomb.* (Author's communication with Michael Simmonds, 27 March 2012)

Once the spring wire was threaded through the hole drilled through the sweet and the detonator attached, the device was immersed in water. When the aniseed ball completely dissolved, a time delay of an hour or so, the detonator would set off the explosives. This allowed the 'frogmen', saboteurs who were to attaching the limpet mines to the side of enemy ships, a safe time to escape before the charges went off. He recalled seeing

> ... quite a lot of this activity going on in the house, particularly this interesting development with an unusual use of aniseed balls. The aniseed balls were drilled and then they were put into little detonator capsules and my father had these ranged around the house and setting off at different times depending on the amount of aniseed ball that was used on each detonator. He would rush into the room in the house where, on the mantelpiece, one of these charges would be put in a big glass Woolworth's tumbler and he would say, 'Right, that's 35 minutes'. It didn't matter that probably the glass had fractured and all the water had gone - he had got something that worked and they were quickly able to establish how much of an aniseed ball was needed to give the varying times of delay that the operators would require. (http://www.bbc. co.uk/ww2peopleswar/stories/34/a5961134.shtml)

Des Turner's research into Aston House, one of SOE's requisitioned houses used for experimental work on explosives, pointed out that,

> The device was tested at Bletchley Park and successfully blew a hole in a barge. The next step was to try it on a moving vessel. A dummy limpet was fixed with magnets to a police launch on the Thames but it fell off, obviously the magnetic system needed to be improved. (Turner, D. (2006), *Station XII Aston House SOE's Secret Centre*, Sutton Publishing, pp.144-45)

Between them, they came up with various improvements

to their invention but, Macrae pointed out,

For safety's or danger's sake, we equipped each limpet with two of three delayed action exploders. The aniseed part of the device had of course to be protected from damp whilst it was in store – and in fact until the Limpet was actually placed on its target. So what we needed was a closed rubber sleeve of some sort which could be pushed over the tube to seal it and whipped off by the Limpeteer when the time came. Again the local shops were able to meet the requirement. We went round to the chemists buying up all their stocks of a certain commodity and earning ourselves an undeserved reputation for being sexual athletes. (Macrae, op.cit.p.11)

During the winter of 1939, Clarke manufactured the first 250 limpets in his Tavistock Street workshop. The second order was for 1,000 so additional space was needed. He bought larger premises in Dean Street, a light industrial area of workshops and garages on the south side of Goldington Road, near the junction with Newnham Avenue.

Nobby and I had done a little costing work on Limpets. His overheads were pretty low, so the asking price came to something like £8 a time out of which he could afford to pay me £2 commission. This was probably more than the profit Nobby was making himself, but he was like that. (Macrae, op.cit.p.20)

As knowledge of their potential spread, further orders came from not just the SOE but the Royal Marines and the OSS who were running a similar training scheme for their saboteurs. As a result of the increased demand, Bassetts, the sweet manufacturers, were given the contract to supply their aniseed balls to a company in Welwyn which was given the contract to manufacture limpets. By the time the war had ended, it had produced over half a million. Turner added that

> Towards the end of the war there was an increasing demand for large quantities of limpets .a search for likely contractors revealed an agency at Elstow, Bedfordshire, that was an experimental filling unit and had no work. The problem then was how to use the unit but not their current workforce. It was eventually agreed that Aston House staff would run the plant and five or six soldiers were permanently installed there until the factory closed after VE day in 1945. they were billeted in the local firemen's accommodation, advised to be on their best behaviour and not to upset the local workers. This went well until their quarters were inspected and it was found that they had much better house-keeping and bed making services. (Turner, op.cit.p.146)

The first use of Clarke's limpet mines was on enemy shipping near Costanza in the Danube but the major success was in Operation Frankton. On 7 December 1942 a team of ten Royal Marines, popularly known as 'The Cockleshell Heroes,' were transported in a submarine, HMS Tuna, to the mouth of the Gironde river, France. Using five, two-man canoes, they paddled by night the 70 miles upstream to the Bordeaux docks. Each man carried several limpets. The Combined Ops website narrates how

> The targets were merchant ships lying in Bordeaux harbour - ships that were successfully breaking the Allied blockade particularly between Japan and Germany. Conventional methods such as bombing had been discounted. Operation Frankton was an unorthodox, imaginative and daring solution. At the end of the first night only 2 canoes and 4 men were still operational. Four nights later they inflicted damage to 5 ships lying in the harbour. Only two men survived and returned to the UK. (http://www.combinedops.com/Cockleshell%

20Heroes.htm)

Other major successes included attacks on ships in Palermo harbour in January 1943, Oslo in April 1943, Singapore in September, Portolago (Greece) and Spezia (Italy) in June 1944 and Jahore Strait (Japan) in July 1945. (Macrae, op.cit.p.221-20)

> *They accounted for hundreds of thousands of tons of enemy shipping and certainly this might be true if the encouraging messages we received by courtesy of our Cloak and Dagger friends and their secret radio stations were anything to go by. Time and time again we would learn that a number of enemy ships had been sunk in harbour by Limpeteers and take off our hats to those brave fellows. One such message was not so good though. It reported that some Italians had got hold of a supply of our Limpets and to date had sunk three of our ships with them.* (Macrae, op.cit.)

During the war years, modifications were made so that Mark III had a spun aluminium bowl instead of the Woolworths' one. The horseshoe magnets were replaced with four large Alcomax magnets designed by Neill's of Sheffield and flexibly mounted so that they could attach themselves to an uneven surface. The aniseed balls were replaced by 'L' Delay fuses. A copper wire attached to the detonator was placed in a capsule of weak acid. When the capsule was broken, the acid would dissolve the wire, setting off the explosive. Different strengths of acid provided different delay times. However, Macrae admitted that

> *This refined model worked no better than its primitive predecessor and oddly enough it never seemed to take on so well with the operators. Maybe this was because it was too refined. True, rubber sleeves were still used to afford initial protection to the 'L' Delays but they were*

now so small that they were useless for any other kind of protection. (Ibid.)

Another weapon Clarke was involved with was the 'Sticky Bomb' which was a grenade which could be thrown at a tank and would stick to it for five seconds or so and then explode, blowing a hole in the tank and, in Macrae's words, 'disconcert the occupants.' There was also the 'W' Bomb, manufactured at Midgely Harmer's engineering works in the Park Royal industrial estate in Wembley, north London. It was a mine designed to be dropped by an aircraft into a river and sink to the bed and remain dormant for a predetermined period. It would then rise to just below the surface and float with the current until it came into contact with a boat or a ship whereupon it would explode with sufficient force to produce a wreck. If it failed to explode after a certain time, it would sink to the bottom and become harmless.

The 'Kangaroo Bomb' and the 'Johnnie Walker' Bomb were variants on this. Upon entering the water the bomb was expected to dive underwater then surface. This would be repeated until it struck the relatively less protected underside of a ship at which point the 90 pound Torpex warhead would explode. (http://en.wikipedia.org/wiki/MD1)

During the spring of 1940, under the direction of Colonel Grand, Royal Engineers, the head of the Secret Intelligence Service's 'D' (Destruction) Section, Clarke was involved in training potential SOE agents in the use of explosives and incendiary devices, for which he was given a commendation. Whether agents visited him in Bedford and practiced in Bedford Baths has not come to light.

Another of Clarke's ideas brought him to the attention of Millis Jefferis, the founder of the Ministry of Supply's unusual weapons section. He had submitted a paper entitled "A consideration of new offensive means", which outlined the design of a large, high-speed trench forming machine.

In a folder in the National Archives headed MOST SECRET and underlined 'TO BE KEPT UNDER LOCK AND

'KEY' was a file entitled 'NAVAL LAND EQUIPMENT'. It details how, in November 1939, the First Lord of the Admiralty approached the Director of Naval Construction to construct a machine to dig trenches at the rate of 5 mph (8 kmph). Instead of large bodies of infantrymen advancing over the surface exposed to enemy fire, there was a plan for them to follow behind a machine digging a trench 7 feet (2.6m) wide and 7 feet deep, wide enough for tanks as well. A sum of £100,000 for experiments was proffered. It was hoped that 200 tank-like excavators might be available by May 1941. Brigadier King, Deputy Engineer in Chief at General Headquarters, ordered a geological survey of the countryside in the north of France and Belgium west of the Dyle River. He was asked to report on the surface and sub-surface soil and rock material down to seven feet. He identified predominantly three to four feet (1.04 - 1.48m) of loam soils or alluvium, covering beds of gravel, clay, chalk, flints, sand and shale similar to those found in Central and Southern England.

Clarke's involvement was found in a letter to the Minister headed 'SECRET'.

> *I have seen Major Jeffries who knows Mr. Clarke. Apparently Mr. Clarke is a man under fifty who runs a small engineering establishment at Bedford and employs 20 to 30 hands, but handles a good deal of other work by sub-contracting.*
>
> *He served as a Sapper in the last War and is apparently a good practical engineer with ideas but not very deep technical knowledge. He has been vetted by M.I.5 and is considered absolutely reliable, making parts of secret machines for Major Jeffries and is at present acting as an Instructor for the training of men for very secret work for the Admiralty.* (TNA AVIA 11/2, 7th May, 1940)

Following an interview in which he outlined his proposals,

a memo was sent to the Admiralty.

> *Memorandum of Interview with Mr. C. V. Clarke*
>
> Mr. Clarke called to see me by appointment this morning. I formed a very good opinion of him. he is frank, direct, obviously knowledgeable, very keen to put his whole weight into the war effort, willing to join the Department as a Temporary Civil Servant, as an Assistant Director at £1,000 a year, willing to allow any question of remuneration for proprietary rights of his inventions to remain over until after the war, does not think that any organisation with which he is connected would be an appropriate one for manufacturing his machine, and understands that the machine would be developed and worked out by us as a Department, free of expense to himself.
>
> I subsequently called in Mr. Hopkins and Mr. McBain, and went over the interview again with Mr. Clarke. Mr. Clarke is to reflect on whether he wishes to bring any staff with him, and whether there are any models for which any remuneration ought to be paid, and will let us have an answer probably by the end of the current week.
>
> Mr. Clarke is 43 years of age. He is connected with the Low Loading Trailer Company, Limited. D.A. Clarke, who signs some of his private letters, is his wife. We are dealing with an individual, and not with a company, partnership, or association. Mr. Clarke is accustomed to secret work, and has access to a special naval school, where certain experiments have been carried out by him. Mr. Clarke is prepared to sign the Official Secrets Act. He was good enough to say that he felt that the interview had been carefully prepared, that all the points which he would desire to have raised had been covered, that he entirely understands the proposal that was being made to him, and had no other points which he in his turn desired to raise at this stage. In answer to Mr.

Hopkins, he said that he would be quite prepared, if it were so desired, to take out a secret patent for his invention. (TNA AVIA 11/2, 8th May, 1940)

Winston Churchill supported his proposals, describing him as 'a man of remarkable coincidences of ideas.' (Ibid.) As a result, in May 1940, he was appointed Assistant Director, Naval Land Section, Ministry of Supply, with a salary of £1,000 a year. Under the directorship of Mr Hopkins, Naval Constructor, his job was to complete the design and construction of these 60 feet long machines. The weight of each machine was 140 tons, and the proposed performance was the capacity to advance through the Siegfried Line, heavily defended German defences running north-south along the their border with Holland, Belgium and France. Clarke's plan was that it laid and fired explosive charges in front of itself so that it could make much quicker progress. He expected it to travel at 200 yards per hour and progress three to four miles in a night. The trench it formed, up to 10 feet wide and 8 feet deep, was big enough to accommodate tanks. A long artillery would be needed during its operation to drown out its noise. Plans were made to build a prototype but on 25th June 1940, France's General Petain surrendered to the Germans, which meant the target disappeared and the scheme was shelved.

He immediately resigned from the Ministry of Supply and notified the War Office of his availability. Called up almost immediately, he signed the Official Secrets Act and was posted to the Intelligence Corps for special duty and joined the SOE staff at their Technical Research and Development Station at Aston House (Station XII), near Stevenage, Hertfordshire.

Aston House was a large country house, set in a secluded five-acre park thirty miles (48km) north of London and only a short drive from Knebworth railway station. It had been requisitioned by the Special Intelligence Services, the covert section of the Foreign Office, in 1939 but was taken over by the SOE. A pond and large chalk pit were used for testing explosives. Bickham Sweet-Escott, an SOE officer, mentioned Aston House in his wartime memoirs, Baker Street Irregular.

Its first commandant was Arthur Langley, a naval commander who won a Victoria Cross and his staff engaged in the design, testing and production of explosives and secret weapons for use in sabotage operations and guerrilla warfare. In Des Turner's book *Station XII,* he described the park as being surrounded by a high wire fence and the locals being told that it was being used to test aircraft flares, special rockets for the Navy and special star-shell fillings for the Army. Staff wore old civilian clothes,, always wore sunglasses and were introduced by fictitious names.

When Clarke first arrived at Aston House 'to sort out a little problem with the Limpet mine,' he did not create a very good impression with his superiors. Macrae mentioned that

Nobby never did stand on ceremony. After waiting five minutes or so at the Guard Post he wandered off and contrived to avoid all security measures and get himself into the house and Langley's presence in another five minutes flat. Nobby relished this kind of exercise and specialised in it later on when he joined the Cloak and Dagger experts himself – first at this station E.S.6 [Experimental Station] and later as O.C. [Officer in Command] of one at Hertford. But although Langley belonged to the same Senior Service he would not wear this one at all. Next day I received a note from him deploring the conduct on behalf of an officer for whom I was responsible. In future, he said, would I please send some officer with some sense of responsibility to Aston House on these missions. If I again sent Captain Clarke he might be admitted to the grounds of Aston House to carry out such work as the testing of Limpets but in no circumstances would he be allowed inside the house and he could not be served with meals. Langley went off a few months later to take a more active part in the war at sea and Nobby then did get into the house for meals. In fact he lived there for several months, having been taken on the strength by Commander Langley's successor – Captain L.J.C. Wood. (Macrae, op.cit.p.94)

Whilst stationed there, agents were also taught the art of silent killing by two ex-Shanghai policemen, Fairburn and Sykes, whose talents were eventually recognised by the OSS who had them transferred to teach their agents in Whitby, Canada. Whether Clarke picked up a few skills from them before they left is unknown. Turner quoted Major Wood detailing how

> We invented, made, supplied and trained personnel in the use of 'toys' not only for the resistance but for all the special forces: Commandoes, Small Boat Section, Airborne Division and Long Range Desert Patrol. We had about forty specialised army officers and civilians, guards and several hundred soldiers, FANYs and ATS (First Aid Nursing Yeomanry and Auxiliary Transport Service—the women's services; by WWII FANY had no nursing connections0 and a few civilian technicians. We had magazines for explosives, and sheds in which to handle them and large storehouses for incendiaries and all the rest of our 'toys', and workshops wherein to experiment and manufacture. We designed and made up special explosive charges tailored for the job in hand and simple to place and fire by any commando or resistance worker. Many tons of explosives as well as devices we supplied were dropped by parachute to the resistance to blow bridges on D-Day. The whole essence of helping the special forces was speed in both invention and supply. (Turner, D. (2006), *Station XII Aston House SOE's Secret Centre*, Sutton, pp.8-9)

Bedford School's Secret Old Boys

When he was not demonstrating or developing explosives, Clarke wrote the 'Blue Book', a manual used by SOE on sabotage technique. Included were instructions on how to use a new light weapon he had invented and produced prototypes for. The existing mortar firing gun had such powerful recoil, his modifications so improved its effectiveness that the Americans purchased large quantities of his 'Tree Spigot'. Their Field Photographic Unit produced an instructional film for OSS agents in which it told them that

The spigot gun was a booby trap or saboteurs weapon for attack against both moving and stationary and moving targets. It is very light and portable and capable of throwing a comparatively heavy bomb with accuracy up to 250 yards. The equipment for spigot gun operation consists of the spigot, the base of the gun, sights for aiming the gun and the bomb which is projected at the target. The spigot has an augur-like handle for setting into the tree or other substantial support and one of the handles is chiselled for scraping away bark. The spigot rod is mounted in the base in a ball and socket joint so it may be aimed and elevated as required. A clamp holds it firmly in the aimed position. The rod contains a spring actuated striker which is held in cocked position by the end of a trip wire inserted in the hole between rod and striker. The sight, similar in principle to a view finder on a camera has range scales in both metres and yards. It fits on the spigot rod while the operator centres the gun on the target before the bomb is attached. The bomb which sits over the spigot rod and is projected to the target is made up of three parts – tail, head and fuse. In the tail there is a shot-gun type of cartridge which when hit by the firing pin of the spigot rod supplies the driving force of the bomb. The silencing rod keeps gases, flames and smoke inside the tail of the bomb making the point of firing very difficult to locate. When the striker in the spigot rod is released by removing the trip wire it springs forward to hit the cartridge in the bomb tail. The exploding cartridge drives the bomb off the rod and the silencing rod and shell peel themselves in the end of the tail preventing the escape of noise and fire. The initial acceleration arms the special fuse so that when the bomb hits its target the impact drives the fuse firing pin into a detonating cap which ignites the booster charge. This booster charge in turn detonates the three pounds of plastic explosive carried in the bomb head. (http://www.realmilitaryflix.com/public/253.cfm)

Time pencils could be inserted when the saboteur felt that they did not need to be present when the vehicle, locomotives, oil storage tanks or building was hit. His 'Plate Spigot' was the same but attached to the gun was a bullet-proof steel plate which screened the firer. Both these weapons were taken on by E.S.6, the War Office as they could also be used by the Home Guard should an invasion ever take place. He also designed a light, portable explosive road trap which was successfully used by SOE and OSS agents. Exactly what it was, was not specified but to give you an idea, the SOE's 'backroom boys' concealed explosives in cavities inside actual everyday objects or in life-size replicas made of plaster or celluloid. These included exploding rusty nuts and bolts, wooden clogs, Chianti wine bottles, screw-top milk bottles, fountain pens, railway fishplates, oilcans, lifebelts, bicycle pumps, food tins, candles, soap, shaving brushes, books, loaves of bread, lumps of coal, rock, turnips, beetroots, stuffed mice and rats and even cow, horse, mule and camel dung!

In December 1940, Clarke was promoted to Captain (Acting Major) and appointed Officer in Charge (O.C.) of Brickendonbury Manor to take over from Frederic Peters. Frank Gleason, an OSS agent, reported how he was sent to an industrial sabotage school in England run by the SOE.

Bedford School's Secret Old Boys

Six or seven people that are properly trained can cripple a good-sized city. It's as easy as can be. These terrorists scare me. If they know this stuff, which I'm sure they do, it's really easy to cripple a medium-sized city with trained demolitionists and arsonists. We learned how to operate and destroy locomotives and power plants, the turbines in power plants, communication systems, and telephones. We also learned how to make people sick by poisoning the city's water supply. Shitty stuff like that – we were taught to fight dirty.

Using a locomotive we learned how to take the controls and get the train moving at a high speed, and jump off – creating a runaway train that would plow into something – isn't that awful? We destroyed rolling stock by removing grease in the gearboxes and putting sugar in gasoline tanks to destroy the engines. We learned how to make explosives from sugar, from basic household supplies, how to start a fire that could take out a city. (McDonnell, P.K. (2004), Operatives, Spies and Saboteurs, Citadel Press, p.7)

According to John Clarke, his father felt it very important that these enthusiastic foreign volunteers should get some actual hands on experience of trying to carry out an attack.

So my father made out a pass on War Office paper saying: 'The holder of this pass, Major C. V. Clarke, has authority to inspect Luton Power Station.' So armed with this pass, which I'm sure from judging the signature which looked remarkably like my father's, he took his team from Hertford to Luton one dark night. They used scaling ladders to get over the walls of Luton Power Station, which of course was guarded like all big installations. They successfully got inside, planted dummy charges on all the transformers, then got back over the wall successfully without anybody noticing.

Bedford School's Secret Old Boys

They, having cleared off to a nearby street and waited for my father who then walked up to the front door of the power station which of course was under guard and asked for the Officer of the guard and produced his pass and he said, 'I want to do a routine inspection.' So he went round with a very big torch and he came up to the first transformer and he flashed his torch and he said, 'What's that?' And this young Subaltern who was in charge of the guard, 'I'm not quite sure what this is Sir.' 'It looks to me like an explosive charge. Let's have a look round.' And in the end the poor Subaltern in charge of the guard was knocked kneed with what he'd let happen. So my father, who was a kindly man said, 'Alright old man, you say nothing about this and I'll say nothing about it. But you've learnt your lesson.' With that he had his team back to retrieve the appliances and off they went. But this was very valuable training, slightly unorthodox but it's one of those things that happened in war time. One of the more wilder outfits in the Army during the war! (http://www.bbc.co.uk/ww2peopleswar/stories/51/a5961251.shtml)

It was common for SOE officers to undertake the same training as the agents. Accordingly, in June 1941, Clarke was sent to Manchester where he attended a parachute course at Ringway Aerodrome. This usually involved five days learning how to jump from increasing heights, land and roll without hurting oneself, put on ankle supports, padded clothing and a sorbo rubber hat, attach the harness and parachute and then make practice three jumps from an air balloon at about 500 feet before two from a converted Whitley Bomber over the nearby Tatton Park. One was at night.

Whilst at Ringway he had an accident which Major Edwards, the Station Commandant, reported on.

I was present on the ground quite near this officer, when he made a descent by parachute, landed rather heavily, and remained on the ground until I came to him with the Medical Officer, who immediately examined the ankle. He was able to walk to the car, and received proper medical treatment. He was on duty at the time, and no personal blame can be attached to him. (TNA HS 9 /321.8)

Three of the agents he taught were flown out of RAF Tempsford on the night of 11th/12th May. Group Captain Hockey and S/L Jackson flew a Whitley to Bordeaux on operation JOSEPHINE. Captain A. Forman, R. P. Calard and Lt. Varnier were parachuted on a mission to blow up the Pessac power station. On reconnoitring the transformer station, they couldn't get past the guards, the 9 ft (2.7 m) wall and the high-tension wire. They also failed to make contact with the submarine which attempted to pick them up on the 20th May. Not to be outdone, they lay low for a month, used specialist gear to climb the wall, open the main gate and set their charges. Six of the eight transformers were blown up. The charges slipped off the other two before exploding and the party escaped.

The disruption to the Bordeaux area took the Germans a long time to recover from. 250 people were reported as arrested, the Pessac area was fined 1,000,000 French Francs and 12 German sentries were shot. Michael Foot, the SOE historian, commented that Mr H.B. Dalton, the Minister of Economic Warfare, contacted Churchill about the importance of the JOSEPHINE mission.

We may therefore take it as practically certain that three trained men, dropped from one aeroplane, have succeeded in destroying an important industrial target. This strongly suggests that many industrial targets, especially if they cover only a very small area, are more effectively attacked by SOE methods than by air bombardment... I hope that with the cooperation of the RAF we shall be able to repeat this form of attack during the coming autumn and winter. (Foot, M.R.D. (1999), The Special Operations Executive 1940 -1946, Pimlico, London)

Whether Churchill acknowledged Clarke's contribution is unknown. John Clarke added that the power station supplied nearby 'U' boat pens from where German submarine left on operations to attack Allied convoys out in the Atlantic. Putting them out of action for several months whilst the power station was being repaired was a major contribution to the war effort. (http://www.bbc.co.uk/ww2peopleswar/stories/97/ a4372797.shtml).

In the summer of 1941, Clarke designed and fitted concealed Spigot guns to a Brixham trawler which was used in SOE operations off the African coasts. Two months after being promoted Temporary Major, in December 1941 he handed over command of Station XVII and joined SOE Headquarters staff as the Officer in Charge of user trials of special arms and equipment.

Another measure of his and Colonel Wood's success at Brickendonbury were the careful planning of SOE missions. Perhaps the most famous was carried out by two Czechoslovakian soldiers, Jan Kubiš and Josef Gabčik. After training using Clarke's newly invented blast grenade on a slow-moving Austin in the grounds of Aston House, they were taken to the airfield. Perhaps there were no flights available at Tempsford that night as they were driven from London to RAF Tangmere, an airfield on the south coast near Christchurch. Their mission was to assassinate Reinhard Heydrich, the Nazi governor of Czechoslovakia, in June 1942. Turner related how

The device was a modified British No. 73 Anti-Tank Grenade. The standard grenade had a tin plate body 9.5 in long and 3.25 in diameter containing 3.25 lbs of Polar Ammon Gelatin Dynamite, a nitro-glycerine-based explosive. The grenade was fitted with the No. 247 fuse

made of black bakelite which is often referred to as the 'all ways fuse' designed to function on impact irrespective of how the grenade landed. Total weight was 4 lb. However, the grenades that Jan Kubiš had to carry were a conversion of the standard grenade made from the upper third portion only. The filling was prevented from falling out by covering the open end with adhesive tape and then binding the whole with tape for added security. The effect of the conversion was to cut the size and the weight to just over 1 lb which would make the device easier to throw and conceal.

[...] there was no limit to the amount of preparation the agents could be given, and it was recognised during the planning of the attack that they would have to seize any opportunity that presented itself . Consequently they took a positive arsenal of weaponry with them including: 2 Colt 0.38 Supers (with shoulder holsters), 4 spare magazines, 100 rounds of ammunition, 4 percussion bombs with PE [plastic explosive], 2 detonator magazines, 2 Mills bombs, (4-second fuses), 1 tree spigot mortar, 1 coil trip wire, 2 igniters, 1 spigot bomb, 1 4-hour time delay fuse for use with 2-lb PE charge, 3 electric detonators and 30 inches of wire and battery, 1 Sten gun, 100 rounds of ammunition, 32 lb PE, 10 lb gelignite, 2 yards of cordtex, 4 fog signals, 3 time pencils, 1 lethal hypodermic syringe. (Turner, D. (2006), Station XII Aston House, SOE's Secret Centre, Sutton Publishing,p.110)

Clarke, as has been mentioned, was also involved in training the agents who undertook the November 1942 attack on Oran harbour in Algeria, where the French Fleet was sunk to avoid it falling into German hands. According to John, he was also involved in the training of six Norwegian saboteurs who, in 1943, destroyed the Norsk-Hydro 'heavy water' plant at Vemork, Rjukan, in Norway, which stopped the Germans from producing a nuclear bomb.

Bedford School's Secret Old Boys

When Flying Fortresses and Lancaster bombers failed to halt production at the Renault engineering works in Lyon that was producing armoured vehicles for the German military, Harry Rée, an SOE agent, trained by Clarke, successfully brought it to a standstill with a few carefully placed explosives. In an interview Rée had after the war, he recalled that

> *The first sabotage was about the beginning of November and they decided they'd blow up a whole transformer house where all the electricity came into the factory. About five men were involved, Frenchmen who worked in the factory. They had their pistols in the pockets of their overalls and they had their explosives, plastic blocks with room for a detonator, in their pockets too. There was a wonderful carelessness about the whole thing. They were playing football with the German guards outside the transformer house—somebody had forgotten to get the key—and in playing football one of them dropped his plastic block of explosive and one of the German guards who was playing football pointed it out to him. 'You've dropped something, sir, I think.' he put it back in his pocket. That was absolutely typical. The transformer house blew up and after they went on throughout the whole of the rest of the war fixing these magnetic blocks to machines and enormously reducing production. (IWM 8688/2; 8720/3)*

The Dunlop tyre factory in Montluçon was similarly disabled in 1944 using two pounds of explosives. Two of Clarke's colleagues who also taught at Brickendonbury, Kim Philby and Guy Burgess, were later discovered to have been working for the Soviet Union. One wonders what sort of report they gave their Russian masters about 'Nobby'.

Amongst the nationalities John recalled his father helping were Poles, French and Dutch. Sometimes he provided them with a brief respite from their training.

Bedford School's Secret Old Boys

I remember as an example of my father's trust in me because I had an uncle who had a farm out at Pulloxhill in Bedfordshire. My father, shortly before an operation was due to take place and before a group of saboteurs were sent off, they having been trained up to the limit and needing a couple of days' break, were sent by my father across to Pulloxhill to help bring in the harvest or do some other job on the farm and it happened that I was there at the same time. My father told me that these foreign people who were on the farm helping my uncle, were saboteurs, that they were going to be dropped over Europe but they were not to know under any circumstances that I was Major Clarke's son. So we kept absolutely quiet about that and worked with them in the field as they were having their break before going on their dangerous missions. (http://www.bbc.co.uk/ww2peopleswar/stories/15/a5961215.shtml)

In February 1942, Clarke requested a transfer to M.D.I. Ministry of Supply, in order to finalise the development and production of his latest sabotage device known as the 'Altimeter Switch'. He visited Macrae at the Firs in Whitchurch, near Aylesbury, Buckinghamshire, another of SOE's requisitioned properties which was described as,

... an ideal place for us. The large house could provide both offices and sleeping accommodation. There was extensive stabling, which could readily be converted into workshops. There were several cottages on the premises and, best of all, included in the property were levelled sites where buildings to serve as stores and so forth could be erected. There were also fields which could be used as firing ranged and where experimental demolition work could be carried out
... What was wanted was a small sabotage device which could be inserted into a German bomber by some brave fellow and would explode when the aircraft

reached a certain height and cripple it ... Nobby Clarke's contribution to this sabotage device was to insist that it should have a flexible sausage of explosive ... In this instance he had worked out that such a weapon as this could not be conveniently concealed in the pocket but could without comment be carried in the trousers. He was wrong about the 'without comment' and there was always considerable ribaldry when he demonstrated this method to his pupils. But actually it was sound common sense and I believe they all adopted it.

In due course we went into production at Whitchurch with this Aero Switch and made and issued many thousands of them. Later by special request we managed to get the operational height down to 5,000 feet without sacrificing the saboteur's safety. The usual drill was to make a slit in the wing fabric of a German bomber and pop this thing inside so that in due course the wing would be wrecked. (Macrae, op.cit.p.88, 155-6)

This 'Aero Switch' or 'Altimeter Switch' was successfully used in numerous SOE operations. After signing the Official Secret Act again, he was appointed Assistant Superintendent and in May 1942, when M.D.I. became a Directorate, its Deputy Assistant Director.

During this time he acted as a Liaison Officer with Imperial Chemicals Industries Limited at their works in Ardeer, in Scotland and Billingham, County Durham. They were involved in the design and manufacture of high explosives and the filling of shells and mortars. One of their inventions which was of interest to Clarke was *'a little 1.7 grain detonator which was only about the size of a percussion cap but instead of needing a blow of 3in/lb to set it off only had to be prodded lightly with a needle point.'* (Macrae, op.cit.p.56) These were used in the 'Clam', a much smaller and more portable version of the Limpet. Macrae claimed that it was their second best seller and that,

Bedford School's Secret Old Boys

For the Cloak and Dagger boys it was God's Gift from Heaven. They could carry these things in their pockets and just stick them to something they would like to blow up. although the explosive content was only around 8 ounces, ICI produced some very high speed stuff for us and the design was such that the explosive was almost in contact with the target over a considerable area. A Clam could put any motor vehicle out of commission or an aero engine for that matter. But its success was dependant on the use of the 'L' Delay which was made part of it. If operators had had to use it with a Time Pencil they would not have been so enthusiastic about it. My diary is full of notes of people squealing for Clams. The Russians had nearly a million of them and were always asking for more. The total number of Clams made under M.D.I. surveillance during the war was over two and a half million. (Macrae,op.cit.p.155)

Macrae used them to produced what he called 'M'-Mines, small explosive devices which he was able to produce at five shillings (£0.25) a time. The ICI detonators were also used in shells designed for another of Nobby's projects, the design and development of the projector for the 'Projector, Infantry, Anti-Tank (P.I.A.T) gun. Although he designed a silencing attachment for the propellant cartridge, the Director General did not consider this necessary when the weapon was used by regular troops.

It consisted of a steel tube, a trigger mechanism and firing spring, and was based on the spigot mortar system; instead of using a propellant to directly fire a round, the spring was cocked and tightened. When the trigger was pulled, it released the spring which pushed the spigot forward into the rear of the bomb. This detonated the propellant in the bomb itself, which was then thrown forward off the spigot. It possessed an effective range of approximately 100 yards (90 m).

This system meant that the PIAT had several advantages, which included a lack of muzzle smoke to reveal the position of the user, the ability to fire it from inside buildings, and an inexpensive barrel; however, this was countered by, amongst other things, a difficulty in cocking the weapon, the bruising the user received when firing it, and problems with its penetrative power. (http://en.wikipedia.org/wiki/PIAT)

Another of Clarke's designs was an auto-release frame system for dropping closely-spaced sticks of small contact bombs from the American Liberator aircraft. This gear was for use with the 35 lb A/S bomb developed by the D.M.D.I. He acted as Liaison Officer with Coastal Command for operational trials. These included 100 hours operational flying with No. 224 squadron based then in Ulster in Northern Ireland and he was involved in one successful attack. With the success of this equipment, he went on to design a similar type of release gear for the Halifax aircraft which were dropping containers of supplies for the resistance movements. (Clarke's Military Record P141671)

John described his father's new posting at,

...a Special Weapon Developments Station set up by Professor Lindemann who became Lord Cherwell, who was Churchill's chief scientific advisor. By this time of course Churchill was Prime Minister and also Churchill had made himself Minister of Defence. The one establishment under the Ministry of Defence that he set up was this research and development weapon station situated just north of Aylesbury in the village of Whitchurch which was code named MD1 Whitchurch, Ministry of Defence 1. My father became Deputy Assistant Director of this secret station where his former colleague Stuart Macrae was already installed and was

Bedford School's Secret Old Boys

in fact Second in Command of the outfit there. It became a very, very big and important enterprise because the great thing about MD1 Whitchurch, which was Commanded by Colonel Jeffries, a Regular Royal Engineer Officer of great distinction.

The thing that made their work different from that of the Regular Army and Ministry of Defence weapon procurement sections was that they had no time whatsoever for red tape. They got things done at twice or thrice perhaps the speed at which the normal procurement method of designing and getting things into production would take. They weren't always terribly popular with some of the Regular Army people who had been doing the job all their Army careers, but they did achieve some very great results.

When my father was in MD1 Whitchurch he was of course carrying on with his weapon development and he devised a system for attacking U boats by air using Liberator aircraft which were used in the later part of the war. It was one of many different types of approach to destroying the German submarines which sailed out of the west coast of France into the Atlantic. His particular contribution was a 35 lb. armour piercing bomb which is quite a small bomb but the thing was that, rather than dropping one or two large bombs from an aircraft at a very small target of a submarine which is rapidly trying to disappear below the waves, it consisted of 20 or 30 smaller charges which were dropped in a scatter device so that they covered a much larger area. Therefore they were more likely to get one of these bombs attacking and actually hitting the target.

My father was attached to Coastal Command for several months flying up and down from St. Eval aerodrome in Cornwall down to Gibraltar and back again in the Liberators and they achieved one or two sinkings as a result of their activities.

Bedford School's Secret Old Boys

One of the chief benefits as far as we children were concerned was we found that my father coming home at weekends from Aylesbury - he occasionally managed to get back to Bedford for a night or two, bearing gifts of bananas and oranges which were totally unknown at that time of the war. (http://www.bbc.co.uk/ww2peopleswar / stories/15/a5961215.shtml)

Training saboteurs, according to Macrae,

... was just Nobby's cup of tea and enabled him to become a bigger menace than ever. He had no guards on the gates of his magnificent estate. One just drove in and then found the vehicle being battered by rounds fired by spigot mortars set off by trip wires. Nobby would emerge smiling and point out that if they had been live rounds the occupants of the vehicles would no longer be in this world. But that was little consolation to the driver who had to explain how the bodywork of his vehicle had been badly bashed.
Nobby made a hobby of raiding the local RAF and transformer stations, leaving his dummy charges all over the place, and then ringing up the fellow in charge to point out that his security measures were lousy. This made him unpopular, and although Colin Gubbins [Head of SOE] liked him he felt that he might be of more use elsewhere. (Macrae, op.cit.p.195)

During the winter of 1943, he visited various weapon training schools and Eighth Army units in North Africa, Italy, Egypt and Palestine to demonstrate the use of the P.I.A.T. and the new 426 fuze to replace the 425 fuze. Whilst in Italy he wrote a rude sonnet on the River Po and

... fell foul of the D of A's representative who was a Brigadier and came home with his tail between his legs. Thoroughly disgruntled, he retired hurt to his Bedford

home without bothering to tell anyone that he was back and I had quite a job to get him out of a Court Martial on grounds of desertion.

After finding a little excitement by going out in Sunderland flying boats from St Eval to see what happened when they dropped our anti-submarine bombs, Nobby returned to The Firs where I tried hard to find him suitable work without much success. When he thought up an idea for a rocket-operated tank bridge it was a great relief to me. It seemed most unlikely the thing would work but developing it would get Nobby out of my hair for a while. So I got [Sir] Millis [Jefferis - his C.O.] to approve the project.

It was quite an impressive one, calling for many men and much equipment. But by now we were quite influential, and I had no difficulty at all in getting a couple of Churchill tanks complete with drivers right away. Nobby got to work, hardly pausing for sleep, and quickly produced some sketches which some genius at G. A. Harvey Ltd of Greenwich managed to translate into masses of girderwork. Large lorries brought this heavy gear to Whitchurch and after we had armed the workshop staff with much bigger spanners they made something of it.

Came the day when Nobby was prepared to demonstrate his creation to one and all. It was a kind of Bailey Bridge carried on the back of a Churchill tank in a folded up position. The idea was that on reaching a canal or narrow river that must be crossed the tank driver halted on the brink of the bank and pressed Button A. This resulted in rockets being fired to throw over the folded part of the contrivance to form a bridge over which tanks could run.

As the pioneer, Nobby of course insisted on being the presser of Button A and nobody else wanted the job anyway. Unfortunately he had not consulted Millis about the mathematics of this venture and had just installed *some 3" rockets to make sure the bridge was thrown over. It was, and it very nearly took the Churchill with it. The driver of the tank was not in a good shape but Nobby remained unshaken and signalled to the driver of another Churchill tank and a Sherman tank who were standing by to climb over his bridge. This the brave fellows did and the viability of Nobby's project was proven.*

The rockets were tamed, and quite quickly Nobby's 'Great Eastern' became one of our show pieces. We used to poop it off and send tanks of all shapes and sizes over it. The big brass loved this, and I had a lot of fun devising means for recovering the bridge reasonably quickly ready for the next demonstration [...] In due course, the first ten Great Easterns were completed and Nobby accompanied them to France after D-Day. They were used and did good work, but unfortunately they were a bit late in the day. If they could have been made available in hundreds it would have made a lot of difference. (Macrae, op.cit.pp.196-7)

His son added that, when the rockets were fired, the upper part lifted 60 feet into the air and that it could be used to cross 12 feet high concrete walls or 30 feet wide rivers or canals.

In the spring of 1944 he commenced the development of the 3rd Mortar jumping ammunition and its fuze which gave a low air burst, a service requirement. He also designed another new type of mortar bomb for air burst ammunition. This was fitted with a high grade explosive and had a manipulated steel tubular body and outer wire winding.

Another idea was a self-propelled multiple mortar firing device for the A43 Churchill tank, known as 'The Black Prince' manufactured by Vauxhall motors. The 17 pounder (76 mm) gun had a maximum rate of fire of 60 rounds a minute.

Whilst his father was engaged in this top secret work, John was kept busy with various cycling adventures. Maybe

Bedford School's Secret Old Boys

'Nobby' joined in on some of them.

...finally in 1944 we went to a much more interesting place in many ways, which was Ledbury in Herefordshire where we were again harvesting but this time plum harvesting and apple harvesting from the fruit crops in the area. These were school parties that were taken out and we camped and had a wonderful time working in the orchards during the day and trying not to get to badly stung by wasps and relaxing in the evenings going out for walks in the beautiful countryside there. So these were really the main holidays that were organised.

But again as I reached the age of about 15 or 16 we used our cycles a great deal. All our 'day boys' in Bedford had cycles because it was very much a town full of cyclists, far more than today. We used to go on holiday with tents and on one occasion, the first time in 1944, we, I and a friend in the Upper School, in September of 1944 we cycled from Bedford up through the Fens to Kings Lynn. And then round the Norfolk coast down as far as into Suffolk and as far as Aldeburgh. I remember the joy of having our first swim in the sea after five years, in Cromer. And another one at Happisburgh a few miles down the coast where you could bathe on a hundred yard stretch between the mined sections of the beaches. As long as you didn't stray, you were alright. On the way back through the beautiful Suffolk countryside we saw the most remarkable sight which was hosts and hosts of gliders being towed for the Arnhem landings in Holland. We didn't know where they were going but it was obvious that there was an extraordinarily large operation taking place. [This was Operation MARKET GARDEN on September 17th, 1944.] We cycled along with our heads in the air, likely to bump into other things because we were constantly looking up to see another team of

Bedford School's Secret Old Boys

planes with gliders behind them, hundreds and hundreds of gliders over this Sunday morning. The whole session took three or four hours to pass and it really was an extremely memorable sight.

Then also the following year with a party of about three other school friends we cycled all the way round Wales. Going from Bedford to the Severn up through wild Wales, up the course of the Wye up to near Snowdon. We then climbed Snowdon, going inadvertently across a live firing range which we didn't really realise it was until we came back again and found that the place that we had crossed at the foot of the mountain was littered with cartridges. Then cycling back through North Wales in beautiful weather and then through the lovely orchard country of Worcestershire and back to Bedford. (http://www.bbc.co.uk/ww2peopleswar/ stories/52/a5961152.shtml

Before the war ended Clarke's Great Easterns had come off the production line and been shipped to Holland. John detailed how afterwards,

My father went out and trained Canadians in the 21st Army Group in the spring of 1945 by which time all the trials had taken place, to use in the latter stages of the war in Holland. The particular use where they felt it could be used was on canals. He trained the Canadians up to a high degree and they were all ready to go to use the bridges across canals, because within 30 seconds or so of the bridge being launched tanks could follow up and cross the bridge and get across what otherwise would be an unfordable obstacle. To my father's private disgust and disappointment, it was ready and planned to carry out an operation at the end of April 1945 when the Germans put their hands up in the Low Countries and the operation was therefore called off. (http:// www.bbc.co.uk/ww2peoples war/stories/51/

a5961251.shtml)

During the war Churchill's 'backroom boys', like Clarke, generated a wide range of weaponry and gadgets but he deserves credit for coming up with so many ideas and developing them. Released from Army Service on 1st November 1945, he went back to Bedford. The family moved to 65 Putnoe Lane and he joined the Territorial Army as Captain for a year before transferring to the Intelligence Corps.

In 1953 the Royal Commission gave him a £300 award for his 'Air Pressure Switch', £400 for his 'Magnetic Bomb (Limpet), but only acknowledged his Magnetic Time Bomb (Clam)' (TNA T166/40)

Stephen Bunker, whose book *Spy Capital of Britain* tells more about Bedford's role in World War Two, described Clarke as a patriot, Land Rover driver, steady smoker, avid reader, member of the Special Forces Club, organiser of the Bedford branch of the Campaign for Nuclear Disarmament and Elder of the Bedford Presbyterian Church. He worked for several years as a Labour Councillor for Putnoe ward before joining the Liberals in 1959, possibly over the nuclear weapons issue. Shortly after retiring as major when he reached the age of 60, he suffered a heart attack and died in 1961.

A week after his funeral, a letter was published in the *Bedfordshire Times* in the name of a number of his friends. It noted that *'his passing is more than just a loss of an individual. To us he was embodiment of an ideal, always in his own way striving after the betterment of society. His vision was broad and embraced all mankind, and he spent himself on its behalf.'* (Bunker, S. op.cit.p.14)

Harold James Andrews (1897 – 1951)
Bedford School OB 1911 - 1914

Harold James Andrews, known all his adult life as 'Mike', was born on 25 May 1897, the son of Arthur Macdonald Andrews, a solicitor in Ulster, Northern Ireland, and Sarah Black, the daughter of an Irish vicar. He grew up at Carnesure, Comber in County Down and his relatives included Thomas Andrew, the shipbuilder who built the Titanic. He attended Mourne Grange School, but, when his father abandoned the family and emigrated to Toronto, Canada, his mother sent him to Bedford, where she had relatives. He started what was then called Bedford Grammar School in the third term of 1911 as a boarder in Paulo Pontine House. With a strong reputation for engineering, perhaps there was a hope that the family saw him following a similar career to Thomas Andrews.

His mother and younger son Ken, came over to Bedford later and lived at 28 Bushmead Avenue, near Bedford Rugby Club. According to Simon Andrews, Harold's grandson, 'with the loss of their father - they never heard him spoken of or saw him again ... one may speculate that this loss and the loss of their tight-knit wider family links and life in Comber, County Down must have profoundly affected these two young boys.' (Email communication with Simon Andrews, 2012)

The only relevant details from Harold's school records were that he was a sapper in the OTC (Officer Training Corps). Following a pilot landing his small plane on the school playing fields sometime before the First World War, Harold, like many other pupils, became fascinated by aviation. In fact, he went on to pursue a career in the air industry.

On holiday in Ireland, he constructed a plane out of wood and canvas on the roof of one of the out-buildings but it crashed on take-off, breaking his cousin's thigh. On leaving school in the summer of 1914, the same year his younger brother Ken started, he was one of the first Bedford School students to get a university degree in aeronautical engineering. During the First World War he started as a fighter pilot in the Royal Naval Air Force, later joining the Royal Flying Corps and flying bombers. Part of his work involved flying biplanes on aerial reconnaissance, taking photographs of the trenches in France, making sketch maps from them and collecting information about enemy airfields and planes in Italy, vital information for Military Intelligence.

He had a wicked sense of humour. His grandson tells of him having a spare joy stick which, when accompanying a student on their first solo flight, he would pull it out of his flying jacket, wave it over his head and, because there was no intercom, indicate that the student behind him had to take over the controls. He was also very lucky, crashing nine times, but. as his plane could only travel at 140 mph, he did not sustain any injuries. There was a story of him flying behind enemy lines in a plane with German markings and a specially modified rear seat in which a passenger could be locked in. He succeeded in tricking someone to climb aboard who was then 'kidnapped' and brought back to base. Earning himself the nickname 'Mad Mike', he was known as Mike ever since. His reputation must have attracted him to the attention of the Secret Intelligence Service, (MI6), for whom he worked over the next few decades. According to his grandson, he was a great fan of Rudyard Kipling and John Buchan and told his family that he worked for the 'Green Hand Gang'.

Based in Lossiemouth at the end of the war, his suggestions helped improve the plane's equipment used to eject torpedoes against enemy shipping and he successfully patented several gadgets for the machine guns used on Royal Naval biplanes.

In 1918 he married Mabel Wright and taught her how to fly, enjoying trips across Europe including arrest and imprisonment in Turkey for landing illegally on one off their airstrips. By 1920, they had two children, Eileen and Harold and in 1922, following the Royal Flying Corps seconding him as an instructor to the Spanish Air Force, he took the family

Captain 'Mike' Andrews, (1897-1951), worked with Spanish Naval Air Force in 1930s, then on clandestine operations for the SIS and SOE in Portugal, Spain and France 1940 – 1944
(Courtesy of Thelwell Collection / Friends of Liverpool Airport)

to Spain and learned Catalan. As well as teaching Spanish students how to fly, he helped design and develop the airbases at Barcelona and Cartagena. In collaboration with Lieutenant Figueras Ballester at the Escuela de Aeronáutica Naval, in Barcelona, in an effort to find the best way of selecting flight staff, he designed a machine which allowed them to measure pilots' reaction times and their errors in interpreting orders. (Bandrés, J. and Llavona, R. *The Militar Aeronautic Psychology in Spain: the pioneers 1911-1925*; http://www.psicothema.com/psicothema.asp?id= 67)

Harold did occasional work for Blackburn Aircraft Limited, one of Britain's naval and maritime aircraft manufacturers, test-flying and demonstrating their aircraft and training pilots in their use. This included Swift torpedo-bombers for the Spanish Navy in 1923/24, which were flown from Barcelona. According to the elgrancapitan website, he was also helpful in modifying Spanish planes so that they could attack submarines.

The Armada had spared no efforts adopting techniques of aerial attack with torpedoes: in 1923 they took on the services of three British instructors to train Spanish pilots in this kind of tactic. In 1923 the contract of one of them was renewed (Navy Lieutenant Harold James Andrews), including among the duties to be done the writing of a report about employment, tactic and use of torpedo planes. (http://www.elgrancapitan.org/foro/search.php?t=18627&sid=359e0dc2e3e9f472d39b806a0d50a49)

Maybe it was in recognition of these achievements that he was elected an Associate Fellow of the Royal Aeronautical Society on 6 September 1925.

During his time in Spain, Mabel taught the children at home. One wonders whether she knew that Harold demonstrated his prowess as a 'crack shot' by shooting a

Bedford School's Secret Old Boys

'Mike' Andrews (right) with Group Captain Hunter RAF (centre) and Frank Court on 30 June 1932, day before the opening of Liverpool Airport
(Courtesy of Thelwell Collection / Friends of Liverpool Airport)

matchbook held in the outstretched fingers of his son.

By 1930, the family returned to England where he continued his aviation career with Blackburn. Aircraft Limited. Throughout this time, he was still working for the SIS, supplying them with sensitive information about foreign air forces, airfields and aircraft gleaned from his flying trips across Europe.

In July 1932, he was given responsibility for the design and construction of Liverpool airport at Speke, (renamed John Lennon Airport in 2002), which he went on to manage until September 1939. In honour of his contribution, Harold's son, Brian, made a bust of his father which was on display in the old Terminal Building. During that time he was a member of the Reserve of Air Force Officers.

When Blackburn discovered that he was involved in clandestine work, he was asked to resign. He then took the Manager's post at Liverpool. Phil Butler, aviation historian and an authority on Speke airport, thought Andrews was 'highly regarded.' According to his communication with Harold's wife, he helped with the design of Kallang, Singapore's first purpose-built civil airport, together with anchorage for seaplanes. Land was reclaimed from a tidal basin to create a circular runway and a slipway for seaplanes. Maybe he was there when it opened on 12 June 1937. According to Butler,

While he was the Liverpool Airport Manager he was involved in meetings and activities with the Air Ministry on various confidential or secret matters. For example, in 1938 or '39, there were secret combined air exercises between the RAF and the French Air Force in which he was personally involved. On the outbreak of war, he left Liverpool almost immediately to take on some post in the Air Force or Air Ministry, of which I knew nothing. ... He part-owned a Blackburn Bluebird biplane [G-AATS] with another Blackburn pilot (Major Higman). Higman owned a property near Biarritz, and Andrews remained in contact with him. Harold's 1939 diary [I have a copy] talks of plans for Harold to fly another aircraft of Higman's to Biarritz in August 1939, but it looks as if the plan remained just a plan. I strongly suspect that Higman was involved in British intelligence work related to the Spanish Civil War. Harold's diary is completely blank after the outbreak of war. (Email communication with Phil Butler, 29 May, 26 June 2012)

Exactly what Harold did during the Second World War has proved difficult to document. His grandson recalled his father telling him that Harold was the Air Attaché at the British Embassy in Lisbon, the capital of neutral Portugal. According to the RAF website, the first wartime Air Attaché to Lisbon, Air Commodore Chamberlayne, succeeded in being repatriated to Britain when war broke out by getting drunk and singing 'Rule Britannia' under the windows of the German Embassy. (www.rafweb.org/biographies/Chamberlayne.htm) However, Lieutenant Commander Philip Johns, the Head of SIS in Lisbon from 1941 to 1943, stated that Wing Commander Jack Shreiber was the Air Attaché when he was there between 1941 and 1942 and that Mike was one of his staff. This was confirmed by Nigel West, the author of MI6: British Secret Intelligence Service Operations 1909 – 45, who described him as a peripatetic fixer sent off on various tasks in and out of the Lisbon office but seems to have been only loosely associated with it. Maybe he was Air Attaché later in the war or told his family that he was as a cover story.

According to the Peerage website, Harold fought 'on special duties' in Lisbon and the Azores, islands off the western coast of Portugal. (Montgomery-Massingberd, H. Burke's Irish Family Records. London, U.K.: Burkes Peerage Ltd, 1976) An Internet search for Mike Andrews, Lisbon and Air Attaché revealed nothing. Changing it to Harold Andrews, I found an interesting article by Ernie Pyle: 'Three Warring Nations Run Planes to Lisbon.' It shed light on the role of the air attaché and also provides insight into what life would have been like in the city whilst Harold was there. All passenger sailings to the United States had been cancelled and the only transatlantic flights were by Wellington bombers from

Bedford School's Secret Old Boys

Newfoundland or by the Pan-American Clipper (Flying Boat) Service. Surprised that the German and British airline company offices were next door to one another, Ernie commented:

Theoretically, the airline to England is a commercial line. But the British air attaché here tells them whom to take, and when. And the air attaché gets his orders from the air ministry in London.

When you arrive from the states, England-bound, you register in a book at the ticket office of British Overseas Airways. That's all there is for you to do. That's all you can do.

Some afternoon maybe a week later, maybe two months later, the ticket office will call up and tell you to get ready. You go when they get down to you on the list. Passengers are chosen in order of their "priority." Nobody goes without priority. This is arranged in London only. The average traveller can't get priority at all.

There are, I understand, seven grades of priority. Highest is for officials travelling on war business – generals, ambassadors, missions and so forth.

I have priority. If I didn't have, I might as well go home. And mine is fairly high priority, too, but when it will get me to London is anybody's guess.

All you can do is wait. Simple waiting is one of the greatest tortures ever devised for man. And it is cold waiting in Lisbon. But it will be colder in London, if that's any comfort for me, which it isn't.

What applies to us, applies to thousands here awaiting transportation. Trains are crowded, The Rome plane is booked three weeks ahead. Time is heavy on people's hands, and as the weeks drag on they draw their financial belts closer and closer.

But at cocktail hour the bars are crowded, and you hear a dozen different tongues. (St Petersburg Times, Monday, 23 December, 1940, p.4)

Bedford School's Secret Old Boys

With Portugal being neutral, like Spain, the hotel bars and the casino had agents from Germany, Vichy France, the Free French, United States, Belgium, Holland, Spain as well as British agents from the SOE, MI6, MI5 and M19. As soon as anyone got out of the plane, their photographs were taken. Everyone was said to have known everyone else.

Another Internet search found the haroldandrews.com website on which were details of what could have been one of the first diplomatic incidents Harold may have been involved with. Following King Edward VIII's abdication and his marriage to Mrs Simpson in 1935, they moved to live in a French chateau and visited other European countries, including Germany. After meeting Adolf Hitler and being honoured by Nazi officials in October 1937, Edward accepted a post as liaison officer with the French government when war broke out in 1939. In June 1940, after France was invaded, he and his wife went to live in Spain. Conscious of Edward's pro-Nazi sympathies and maybe aware of the German Foreign Minister, Joachim von Ribbentrop's plans to return him to Britain as a puppet king with Lloyd George's support, Winston Churchill and George VI wanted him out of the way and offered him the Governorship of the Bahamas. Hitler and Ribbentrop recruited Walter Schellenberg, who had a large spy organisation across Europe, to locate and kidnap the couple and take them to the German Embassy in Madrid. The SIS learned of the plot, posted guards around the villa near the Spanish frontier where the couple were on a hunting trip, and spirited them to Lisbon before the Nazis arrived. One imagines the air attaché receiving orders to ensure that they were put on the first available flight out of Portugal on 1 August 1940. (http://www.forum.haroldandrews. com/ubbthreads.php/topics/88448/9; Deacon, R. *A History of the British Secret Service,* Frederick Muller, London, (1969),pp.291-2)

Philip Johns, using the cover as Financial Attaché, described 'Mike' as having 'no specific duties but could be called upon to carry out any outside missions which might arise.' (Johns, P. *Within Two Cloaks*, William Kimber, 1979), p.74) Only one such mission has come to light. The SIS in Lisbon was on an intelligence gathering mission for the British Government which was concerned about Hitler planning to invade Spain and Portugal. Following Germany's success in capturing Holland, Belgium and France in May 1940, there were real worries that the Nazis were planning to invade the Iberian peninsula and attack the British colony of Gibraltar. Once crossing the Pyrenees, it was thought that, after the recent two and a half year long Civil War, .the Spanish army would not be able to put up strong opposition to any Panzer divisions. According to Johns, the British Admiralty needed information on

'the locations and movements of enemy surface vessels, particularly the so-called pocket battleships, and just as important, the German U-Boats; construction of enemy ships, particularly U-Boats, and the development of newer and larger submarines; activities in the various ports of occupied countries, Rotterdam, Antwerp, Copenhagen, Oslo; details of cargo carried, particularly in the Baltic, between Germany and Sweden and coastal defences in the Channel by the Todt organisation.

The War Office was primarily interested in the disposition of enemy units and particularly any significant movements from the west to the east fronts. Agents were to be briefed for the identification whenever possible of the regimental 'flashes' worn on shoulder or arm. It was particularly important to know what units, armour, and armament were being deployed along the western coast of France.

The Air Force questionnaires were directed to details of aircraft losses in the Luftwaffe, bombers and fighters, current production to replace losses and to reinforce German strength in the air; any new types of aircraft; training of glider personnel and paratroopers, construction of new airfields, again particularly in the region of the English Channel as a threat to our own eventual D-Day of Liberation.

Bedford School's Secret Old Boys

The Ministry of Economic Warfare required information as to shortages of food and material resulting from the blockade of Germany; deliveries of wolfram from Portugal and Spain; steel production and steel deliveries from Sweden and from occupied Europe; oil deliveries from Rumania and the USSR; synthetic rubber (Buna) production; the general state of health in Germany itself and the occupied countries, with current information regarding rationing and clothing.' (Ibid.p.75)

According to his grandson, Harold had to fly people on diplomatic and other missions and used his flights up and down the Portuguese coast and across to Azores to collect intelligence. Johns mentioned Commandant José Cabral, an officer of the Portuguese Air Force, and in 1941 a senior pilot of TAP, the Portuguese commercial airline.

It was here that Mike Andrews on my staff became indispensable. ... He was also an air force officer, a flight lieutenant, tall, almost gaunt in appearance and, although I have never heard him complain, I was under the impression that his health was far from good. He had great charm and personality and available for any mission outside the office. He was almost a professional photographer and was a friend of José Cabral, who captained the regular TAP flights from Lisbon to Tangier and Casablanca.

One of my high priorities was to keep a close watch on the extended Portuguese coastline as the Admiralty suspected that some of the smaller harbours might be providing sanctuary and victualising facilities for enemy U-boats. José was approached and without any hesitation agreed to take Mike Andrews on one of these flights to Morocco, to install him in the cockpit of the aircraft, and to arrange his flight path in such a way as to allow Mike to take a series of photographs as close to the coastline as possible. The resulting series of photographs were excellent. There were no signs of any enemy craft, but the admiralty found the pictures of great value, and they enabled us to arrange for coast watching at various points which seemed potentially capable of sheltering German submarines. (Johns, op.cit. 98-9)

One upshot of this mission was the establishment of a Vice-Consul at Faro, on the Algarve coast where coast watching duties were undertaken. One imagines that Harold also monitored activity in and around Portuguese and Spanish airports.
Whilst In Lisbon, Harold, like other British diplomats, would have had to pay serious attention to the unofficial directive that they had to be prepared, at short notice, to leave the Portuguese capital. All British diplomats in Portugal were ordered to keep a knapsack in their bedroom, packed with warm clothing, tinned food and medicines. Should the invasion happen, he had to make his way to the docks where an ocean-going tug moored in the Targus, was ready to rescue British diplomats and take them to North Africa.
Although Spain was described as neutral, some British officials preferred to describe it as non-belligerent. Franco's government officially 'regretted' attacks by Italian naval saboteurs on the British port facilities at Gibraltar. Hundreds of Germans and German agents were allowed to move freely about Portugal and Spain and the Luftwaffe's 'emergency' use of Spanish airfields was a constant worry for the British Admiralty as Spain's long Atlantic and Mediterranean coastlines allowed attacks on Allied convoys. One imagines that Harold would have had to monitor German activity in Lisbon and the rest of the country and report back to London.
When I contacted the British Embassy in Lisbon to query whether they might have any information on Harold, they replied that the Ministry of Defence had told them that, because the British do not have a Military attaché in Lisbon today, any relevant files would have either been destroyed or deposited in the National Archives in Kew. Imagine my

surprise when I found one on their online catalogue with a Special Operations Executive (SOE) reference number and then my disappointment when they told me it was 'closed', not available for public viewing. On making enquiries using the Freedom of Information Act, I was told that I needed to provide a copy of his birth certificate to prove that he was over a hundred, a death certificate or an obituary. Graham Ward, one of the Friends of Liverpool John Lennon Airport, helped by sending me proof of his death, which I forwarded to the National Archives. They agreed to 'open' the file but when it was examined there was only a single folio stating that he was employed by the Special Operation Executive's H (Iberian) Section under commercial cover. (TNA HS 9/36/6)

A further search located a reference to an H18 file, a nominal index of SOE contacts in Spain, Portugal and North Africa. Checking the online catalogue for information about it, my hopes were raised when I read that the cards give the name and, where known, contact details for SOE personnel and contacts, any aliases used, sometimes biographical details and information about the subject's usefulness to SOE, plus details of any operations they were involved in or escape lines they were linked to. It added that many of the cards relate to SOE contacts with experience of Iberia though currently based in the UK. However, my expectations were dashed when I read that the index was incomplete – the first surviving card is under the name of Jose Maria Betazom, and the fate of the earlier alphabetical cards is not known.

According to Simon Andrews, Harold told his family that he posed as a migrant Spanish worker, crossing the border into France where he stayed in safe houses, sometimes sleeping in ditches and helping with an escape line. Following the evacuation of Dunkirk at the end of May 1940, an estimated 60,000 Allied troops were left behind, Whilst many surrendered, others were captured. Some who evaded capture or who were helped escape prison, with the assistance of dedicated members of the resistance, made their way south to the Pyrenees in order to escape into Spain.

Bedford School's Secret Old Boys

When few were fluent in French, some brave individuals went out of their way to help them make the journey. Over time more men, following instructions, escaped from prisoner-of-war camps and prisons and found people willing to help them return to 'Blighty' to fight another day. There were also civilians, men and women who wanted to escape from under German occupation and, as the war progressed, increasing numbers of Allied aircrews who had either parachuted from a burning plane or managed to survive when it was shot down.

Many Dutch, Belgian, French men and women working for the resistance, often secretly funded by wealthy supporters, provided old clothes, food, safe houses and forged travel documents to help get people back across the Channel, over the Alps into Switzerland, or south to Marseille or Toulouse. Here there were small groups of British and Allied sympathisers willing to provide accommodation, food and onward travel. On moonless nights, often after midnight, some evaders were escorted to a remote beach where they were met by men in rowing boats who picked them up and took them to a boat or submarine waiting offshore. Most however, were escorted by bus or train to the foothills of the Pyrenees to await a 'passeur' a French or Spanish guide, who would take small groups over one of the high mountain passes and down into Spain.

Depending upon where they crossed the Pyrenees and the time of year, the journey could d be several days. According to Donald Darling,

> *Those who only know these famous mountains by name, could be forgiven for not appreciating what a barrier they form between France and Spain. Many of the rugged peaks are over ten thousand feet high and their rocky foothills, which sprawl into both countries, are more than heavy going for the average hiker. Snow lasts well into July and forms again in October. At each extreme (Biscay and Mediterranean), the mountains are easier to cross, and the time taken by a group of fit men*

Bedford School's Secret Old Boys

is about ten hours, though many valleys have to be crossed from side to side to avoid police posts on the roads below. To men not in good condition and perhaps ill-shod, such a journey could become a nightmare of exhaustion and pain, though, spurred by the hope of getting to safety, most groups somehow managed to endure it. (Darling, op.cit.p.98)

Learning of these escape lines, the Germans increased controls along the frontier, making the journey more dangerous. They also tried to infiltrate these lines, trying to send one of their own agents posing as an evader, and offering large financial rewards to anyone who could provide information leading to the arrest of the escaped prisoners-of-war, aircrews or evaders as well as the people who escorted them, the guides, those who provided safe houses and especially the organisers.

Armed German guards patrolled the border with Alsatian dogs, on the look-out for groups of 'evaders'. The Spanish police were also aware that there were people entering the country illegally. Those who were not caught, depending upon where they crossed the Pyrenees, were taken to the nearest British Consulate at Bilbao or Barcelona. That was not the end of their journey. Having been checked by British officials they would have been provided with a salvoconducto, a document allowing onward travel to Madrid, from where arrangements were made for them to be taken, sometimes in the boot of a car, across the border into Portugal if they were civilians or Gibraltar if they were in the Armed Forces. (http://www.rafinfo.org.uk/ rafescape/guerisse.htm)

Those who were caught in France were often imprisoned and interrogated. Some ended up in concentration camps and either died, were executed or liberated. Those 'illegal immigrants' caught in Spain were arrested and imprisoned, initially at Figueras, close to the French border, before being transferred to prisons in Saragossa, Barcelona or the 'Campo de Concentracion' at Miranda de Ebro near Burgos.

People claiming that they were evaders were often released, sometimes after a contribution to the appropriate benevolent fund had been paid. MI9 was not averse to bribery to avoid arrest or ensure escape.

When it cost £10,000 to train an RAF pilot, rather than train new pilots, it was economically worthwhile to provide some form of financial reward for getting downed pilots and others back to Britain. Smugglers were willing to guide people into Spain for a few thousand francs a head. Later in the war, following the arrest and execution of some of those involved, some 'passeurs' would only accept gold sovereigns. According to Michael Bentine of MI9, well over 2,000 evaders, mostly Allied aircrew, were got out. 'Pilots cost rather more than a navigator, then came a flight engineer and a bomb aimer. Way down on the list in cost came air-gunners who took the shortest time to train.' (Michael Bentine, 'It's a Mad Mad Mad Mad War, BBC Radio 4 Extra, 8 July 2012) Pilots had a price tag of 5,000 francs. This money came through the Embassy hidden in cans of 35 mm film and it is very likely that Harold was involved in this clandestine activity. To cover this operation, Bentine joked that there was an endless film festival in Lisbon during the war.

What was called 'courrier' was brought down the escape lines. This was handwritten or typed documents, photographs, annotated maps, sketches, anything containing information which the resistance organiser could not transmit by wireless. Often brought hidden in a tube of toothpaste, a rectal container or, if confident they wouldn't be searched, strapped in a pouch around their body, it was handed over to British Embassy staff to check over and decide whether it was to be sent direct to London on the next plane or, to be encoded and transmitted by wireless immediately. Maybe this was one of Harold's tasks.

Having lived in Spain for years, he was fluent in Catalan and with his dark hair and one imagines tanned skin, he would have passed as a Spaniard. He reported having to sleep in ditches and, on more than one occasion, looking down the barrel of a gun. Given that he was engaged on secret work for the SOE, it is not surprising that details of his activities have not been documented. However, some MI9 officers had their wartime autobiographies published in the 1970s, which shed light on their work with the escape lines. Whilst they do not mention Harold, one imagines Her Majesty's Government ensured that no sensitive data was allowed to be published.

Donald Downing, an intelligence officer with MI6, was transferred to MI9 and, like Harold, was posted to Lisbon. Code-named 'Sunday', his title was British vice-consul in charge of refugees, a cover for supporting the escape lines. Initially this involved providing financial assistance, arranging for messages to be taken to various members of these resistance groups in France but later arranging for wireless sets and wireless operators to be sent in.

He was involved, as might Harold might have been, with the collection of 'refugees' from prisons, the Consulates and Embassy in Spain and arranging their transport across the borders into Lisbon or Gibraltar in the boot of one of the diplomatic cars. Maybe Harold carried some in his Model T Ford, which he had modified with a more powerful engine. Darling was also involved in debriefing the evaders. As this numbered over two thousand, he had assistance and, in his autobiography, Sunday at Large, he admitted that,

> *My Intelligence colleagues and I, as a group, became known ... as 'The Funnies', since no other blanket description of us seemed to fit. Newcomers did sometimes ask that dreaded wartime question, 'What do you do?' In order not to be downright rude, I used to reply, 'Oh, this and that', and the hint was usually taken. I suppose that had I replied, 'I've met some Germans off a plane from Cairo at midnight' or 'I have to collect a French secret agent in the dawn and put him up in the flat', I would have been put down as a 'bloody liar'.*

Nevertheless, it could have been true. (Darling, D. Sunday at Large, William Kimber, (1977), p.12)

One of the people put up in Lisbon was Airey Neave, who had escaped from prison in Colditz Castle and brought down the escape line. He ended up working as another MI9 officer in Lisbon with the code-name 'Monday'. 'Saturday' was Michael Cresswell, a British Embassy official in Madrid. Undoubtedly, Harold would have had dealings with them.
Harold's official' job was in the Passport Office, the common cover in the diplomatic service for clandestine activity, and he told his son that he developed a second sense about people coming through acting strangely. This supports the idea that he was in liaison with MI9, vetting the men and women coming to Lisbon from the escape lines.
Whilst in Portugal he had a code book and made an arrangement with his son who had a copy of Erskine Childer's 1903 spy novel, *The Riddle of the Sands*. Having a photographic memory, Harold had memorised a few pages and used key words from it to send coded messages home on postcards to assure his family that all was OK. (Email communication with Simon Andrews, 4 July 2012)
it is possible Harold liaised with Captain Ian Garrow and 'Pat O'Leary' (real name Albert-Marie Guérisse), whose 'PAT' line helped evaders get out of France from their base in Marseille. He probably also liaised with Andrée de Jong, a young Belgian woman who helped start the Comète line.
In keeping with his reputation as an action man of 'derring do', his grandson recalls a story where Harold kidnapped one of the German Ambassador's many cats, shaved its fur, drew swastikas on it and put it back. Philip Johns described an incident when he and a group of friends, including Harold, went into Restaurant Gambrinus, just off the Avenida de Libertade.

Nearby at a corner table across the room was a party of Japanese, accompanied by a German Abwehr official. We had dined well and at the end of our meal when we were lingering over our coffees, Mike, without saying a word to any of the rest of us, bowed politely, saying, 'May I have the pleasure of welcoming you all to Portugal and at the same time to express my own personal admiration of the magnificent victories of your famous Generalissimo Chiang Kai Chek.' He bowed again very correctly and came back to rejoin our party. The Japanese were obviously taken aback, too much so to have any immediate reaction. I seem to remember that they even bowed as Mike walked away. I never knew if any of them spoke English well, but I am quite sure that their German companion did, and it must have been explained to them the implications of the welcome speech of Mike Andrews, because they all glared at him later and the atmosphere became very frigid. (Johns, op.cit.pp.99-100)

In the family photograph collection there are a few of him attending a party at one of the 'Port' family's homes. There were long standing British families engaged in the export of port. According to his grandson, this particular family was involved in resistance work. I tried contacting Cockburn, Croft, Dow, Gould, Graham, Osborne, Offley, Sandeman, Taylor and Warre. Only Sandeman responded but said that no-one had heard of him.

When Darling was posted to Gibraltar in January 1942, part of his job involved interviewing all the evaders prior to them being sent to Britain. Maybe Harold passed on information about those he came into contact with. Following a large number of arrests in the Marseille area, there were suspicions that some members had been coerced under torture or tempted by the rewards the Gestapo was offering to provide names and addresses of people in the resistance. One imagines that when posters were stuck up everywhere informing readers that the death sentence would be issued to anyone helping downed aircrews as well as those who failed to denounce those involved, some people were persuaded to collaborate.

Harold must have made many useful contacts in the Spanish Air Force during the many years he lived in Spain and have had insight into their political views of Franco, Hitler and Mussolini. One imagines he developed contacts within the Portuguese Air Force.

According to Simon Andrews, Harold, dressed as a Spanish migrant labourer and sometimes sleeping in ditches, made contact with members of the French resistance, identified safe houses and presumably took money to support those involved in the escape line. It was a highly dangerous occupation as the Gestapo were aware of the escape lines and, over the course of the war, managed to infiltrate some and destroy them.

It is quite possible that he was involved in negotiations for the release of those captured by the Spanish authorities. If he had his own or an embassy car, the CD diplomatic plates would have facilitated easy passage through Spanish police controls. He could have used it to pick up evaders from the Pyrenees, from the consulate in Bilbao or Barcelona and drive them to the British Embassy in Madrid. Here fake identity papers and travel passes were issued before their onward travel either to Lisbon or to Gibraltar, where Darling had the task of interrogating each and every one to ensure they were 'bona fide' evaders. Once he was satisfied, depending on how important they were, they were sent back to Britain in a naval convoy or by plane.

Enquiring with the Embassy in Lisbon as to whether they had any information about the time Harold spent with them, I was told that the Ministry of Defence had told them that, as Lisbon no longer has a resident Defence Attaché, the documents would have either been destroyed or transferred to the National Archives. On searching their catalogue I found his file in the SOE's personnel section – except that it was closed. (TNA HS 9/36/6) With the assistance of Graham Ward, I provided the National Archives with proof of his death, which allowed access to the file. It was a one page document with his name. There were no forms, no training reports, no correspondence, no telegrams, nothing. The SOE had a team in Lisbon, code-named 24-Land. Maybe he did occasional work for them. (Email communication with Jose Antonio Barreiros, 2012) However, according to Darling,

> *Protocol demanded that diplomats may not indulge in clandestine activities or use their diplomatic immunity to further such ends. It was clear that the traffic of evaders through Spain was an embarrassment to the Embassy in Madrid yet, obviously, as it increased and became a steady flow, it was of great importance to the war effort and therefore had somehow to be endured by diplomats.* (Darling, *Secret Sunday*, p.56)

Maybe Harold drove thousands of miles in his diplomatic car with its protective diplomatic plates to pick up evaders from the consulate in Bilbao or Barcelona. To avoid going through the same Spanish police controls on a regular basis, he would have had to vary the routes he took. Darling admitted that there was some police superintendents had guessed what was happening in the Barcelona area but, being sympathetic to Britain, they took no action. Such official blindness could not be relied upon across Spain and there were certainly cases where bribery had to be used. One imagines Harold might have had to carry large sums of moneys, possibly including gold sovereigns, to undertake his clandestine work. Darling estimated several thousand men and women were brought out of France between 1940 and 1944, describing it as changing from being 'a skeleton in the Embassy's cupboard to becoming a feather in the Ambassador's Homburg'. (Darling, op.cit.pp.56-8) The record from being shot down over Belgium to being back in England was ten days.

During the years he spent in France and Spain, Harold caught tuberculosis and was returned to England in 1944.

Bedford School's Secret Old Boys

Financially, he was in dire straits. His brother Ken, also a Bedford School Old Boy, tried unsuccessfully to obtain a pension for him. The RAF maintained that he had not been working for them. One imagines that the SIS neither confirmed nor denied that he worked for them. Ken cared for him and paid the medical fees for treatment in Davos in Switzerland. This was before the National Health Service and before the introduction of streptomycin, a drug to treat TB. When slightly better, he was appointed the first warden of Speke Hall, the Tudor half-timbered property near Liverpool airport but he died in Aigburth on 10 June 1951.

Charles Barton Bovill (1911 - 2001)
Bedford School Old Boy (1918 – 1925)

Charles was born on February 18th, 1911 at Battersea, south London, the second son of Ethel and Charles H. Bovill. His father was a successful playwright who wrote the lyrics for five musicals and employed a youthful P. G. Wodehouse (1881 – 1975), the successful English comic novelist, as an assistant. Wodehouse was famous for his humorous accounts of life in upper-class English society featuring Bertie Wooster, the eccentric aristocrat and Jeeves, his butler. They had several short stories published in the Strand in London and in the Pictorial Review in the United States and a number of plays running in theatres in the West End of London.

He was brought up at The Knowle, a 17th century cottage in Barcombe, a small rural village in Sussex between Brighton and Eastbourne, and attended Revd. E. Griffith's Grammar School in Lewes.

Following the outbreak of the First World War in 1914, his father served as a Lieutenant but, like millions of others, was killed fighting on the Western Front. Ethel, his mother, took the boys to Bedford and found accommodation at 32 Clapham Road. Whether she already had connections in the town is unknown. Edward, Charles' nine-year old brother, started at Bedford Preparatory School in September 1918 and he started the following year when he was seven. Charles' school record shows he was put in the 4th Division of Year One. Numerous absences were noted, attributed presumably to a note that he had a "weak heart." In fact, he was abroad for the whole of 1923.

According to his obituary in *The Daily Telegraph*, Charles was sent to the Mediterranean coast of France to be brought up by his aunt, a formidable character who, it was said, was well known to Wodehouse. Several of his aunt's traits were included in Wodehouse's fearsome character, Aunt Agatha, who "eats broken bottles, wears barbed wire next to the skin and offers human sacrifices at the time of the full moon." (*The Daily Telegraph,* 9 May 2001)

Whether his experiences with this "nephew crusher" convinced him that he had to return to school is unknown, but his records show that he restarted in 1924. He joined the Mathematical group, as opposed to the Classical, and progressed to the 2nd Division before leaving at Easter 1925 when he was only fourteen.

The 1920s saw a craze in making what were called 'crystal sets'. These were do-it-yourself radio kits, as pre-assembled models were not then available. Charles's Science teachers at Bedford School probably encouraged him to read the popular Science magazines that could be found in the library or bought in shops in the town. In many of them he would have found instructions of building a crystal set. Maybe he made one in lessons?

Boy Scouts, very popular in the 1920s, had lessons in making them. Should he or his teachers have smoked they could have found instructions on printed cards found inside every pack of Philip Godfrey cigarette packets. These sets used an antenna wire wrapped around a Quaker Oats or other cereal packet, and were tuned by touching a 'cat's whisker' or diode to a mineral crystal. The radio waves could then be listened to using early headphones.

Edward was more academic at school. He left Bedford the following year when he was seventeen and followed his father's military footsteps, being accepted at the Royal Military Academy at Sandhurst, in Surrey with a Prize Cadetship. In 1928 he joined the Royal Tank regiment but died four years later of typhoid fever in Peshawar, close to what is now the Indian/Pakistan border in the Punjab.

Where Charles went after leaving school is unknown, possibly back to France, as he went on to study radio at the University of Grenoble and then at Regent Street Polytechnic in central London. When he graduated he did not get a job working with radio straight away. He found employment in the meat trade in the Smithfield area of the city. But it was

Bedford School's Secret Old Boys

Charles Bovill, Marconi radio expert during World War Two.
(Courtesy of Klas Nilsson)

not his choice of career. As a young man in the 'swinging twenties' he needed money. In an interview he gave in 1994 to Klas Nilsson, the Chief Executive Officer of Security Manager, Sweden, he shed light on what happened after he left.

We were pretty poor when I started this business. I used to carry meat around from this meat market, and I didn't like it. And I used to go home every weekend to a place called Bedford, to see my mother and to keep an eye on her. One day I met a man much older than I was, who asked me what my job was. So I told him that I wanted to get into electrical engineering and had studied radio at the University of Grenoble in France. This was a very long time ago, 1928. He said, "Forget the meat market. I will give you a job. Get a few books about electricity and start with me next month." I had two enjoyable years with him. I will not go into the reasons I left. But in 1933 I was not working and went down to the motor racing course at Brooklands [near Weybridge, Surrey] where I met an old school friend and told him of my hope of getting into radio. To my surprise he said go and see my brother at His Masters Voice. [HMV had a factory in Hayes, Middlesex.] I went and was very happy there developing domestic radios. Learned everything I wanted to. I went to night schools two or three times a week. The war was by then in the offing and I was offered a job by the Air Ministry as an inspector of RAF radio equipment. [The Royal Air Force had their headquarters at Adastral House on Kingsway, London.] I was awfully bored and they did not like me and I did not like them. I must be able to do something. I didn't like to waste my talents. I applied for a job in the Air Division of Marconi's and got it. The date was January 3rd 1938 and was one of the great days of my life.

Bedford School's Secret Old Boys

The Knowle, Barcombe, Sussex, a 17th century cottage where Charles Bovill spent part of his early childhood.

http://www.bandhpast.co.uk/barcombe/b0428build.php 11th January 2010)

Front covers of one of Charles' father's collaborations with P. G. Wodehouse.

Bedford School's Secret Old Boys

Everything went perfectly for me. (http://securityriskmanagement.eu/content1.asp?cID=charlesbovill-en 12th December 2009)

The Marconi Wireless Telegraph Company had a radio factory in Chelmsford, Essex. Whilst there he probably met Christopher Cockerell, a senior engineer with Marconi from 1935 to 1951, who was later given a knighthood for his invention of the Hovercraft. Charles' work involved working with the radio equipment that Marconi sold to civilian aircraft companies.

As war approached, Marconi arranged for Charles to go and work with RAF Bomber and Coastal Command as a wireless development engineer where he had to liaise between them and the company. He was aware that the existing radio equipment on the RAF's planes was of a very old design. After the first bombing raid of Germany in May 1940, it became apparent to Charles that the RAF needed more up-to-date radio equipment.

Marconi was asked to carry out trials with all RAF bomber types using the company's latest model which was already fitted to many of the country's civilian aircraft. Charles carried out all the tests on what he called AD77. According to the Duxford Radio Society, this was one of Marconi's existing transmitters. Following these checks, he supervised the fitting of hundreds of Hampden, Blenhiem, Whitely and Wellington bombers and made many test flights in them. By 1945 Marconi had made about 30,000 of these sets for Bomber Command.

Following the German invasion of France and the Low Countries on 15th May 1940, Marshal Petain, the French military leader, signed the Armistice. In the summer of 1940, the Secret Intelligence Service (SIS), the covert section of the Foreign Office, approached the Air Ministry with the suggestion that they experiment into how feasible it would be to parachute agents and land aircraft into enemy territory to pick up and bring back VIPs (Very Important Persons). They

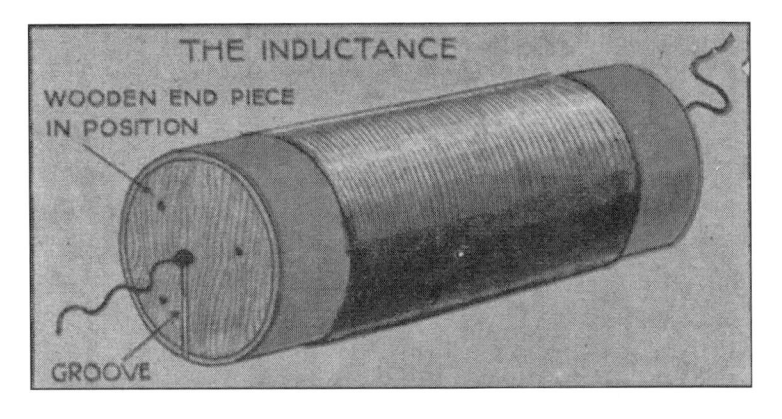

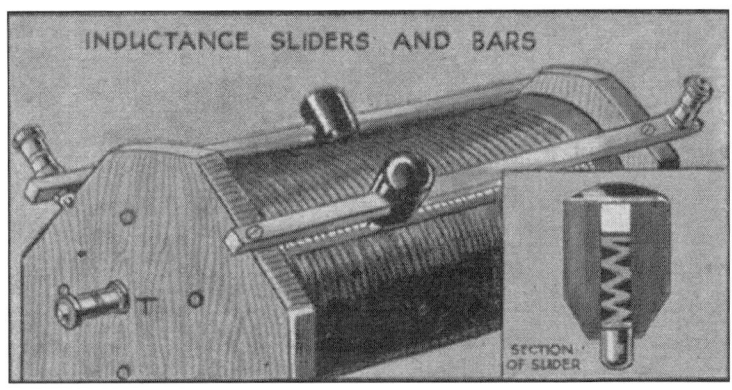

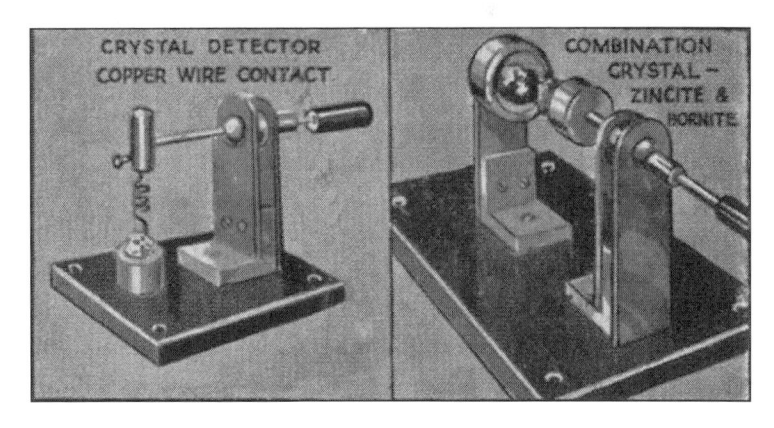

Cards issued with Godfrey Phillips Cigarettes in the early to mid-1920s which were very likely collected by Bedford schoolboys., (www.r-type.org/static/crystal.htm 10th January 2010)

recognized that they would be very useful with the Allies' war effort. Many military and diplomatic personnel had been left behind after the evacuation from Dunkirk at the end of May. Some merged into the local population and helped train them clandestinely to oppose the German assimilation of the conquered territories. It was essential that some of these people needed bringing back to England occasionally for additional training and then sent back with funds to support the various resistance groups.

The urgency of the situation was taken on board and Winston Churchill, the British Prime Minister, set up the Special Operations Executive (SOE) with a directive "to set Europe ablaze." Their operations were to be 'unattributable' industrial sabotage, the raising and supplying of secret armies and collecting intelligence information, all done under what Michael Foot, the SOE historian, described as "the dense fog of secrecy." Those 'in the know' called it the Inter-Services Research Bureau (ISRB). Its five-floor office block at 64 Baker Street in London was just down the road from the flat occupied by Sherlock Holmes, Sir Arthur Conan Doyle's fictitious detective,

Given the nature of its work, the SOE Headquarters had to have War Department cover so the name MOI (SP) was coined and its telephone number added to the War Office's directory. Captain Peter Lee, an officer in its security section, was quoted as saying that "it was terribly clever. *We said it stood for 'Mysterious Operations in Special Places'. We reckoned the Germans, with their lack of sense of humour, would never be able to unravel that one."*

London gradually introduced clandestine operations into occupied Europe in an attempt to destabilise the German forces. Under the cover of night, some secret agents were taken by boat or submarine and dropped on isolated beaches. Important military, political and commercial personnel were returned safely to south coast ports but, as the Atlantic Wall, an extensive network of coastal fortifications stretching from Norway to Spain, was completed, this method

Bedford School's Secret Old Boys

Listening to a radio set in the 1920s was a new experience. Boys were keen followers of this new technology.

(1920s.www.wired.com/.../2008/09/radio_1921_630px.jpg 10th January 2010)

So were girls. An early-1920s radio set with a 'scientific appearance' from an original painting by Jenny Nystrom.
(http://www.historyofpa.co.uk/gfx/cw/2lo/girl.jpg 4th February 2010)

became increasingly dangerous.

1419 Special Duties Squadron, operating from Newmarket racecourse in Cambridgeshire, flew out on the few nights available between the waxing and waning of the moon to drop agents and supplies into occupied Europe. Pilots had to fly low, often below 100 feet (37m) above sea level, to avoid enemy radar. They did not use lights so they could avoid the attention of the people manning the searchlights and flak batteries. (The word flak comes from the German Fliegerabwehrkanone, aircraft defence cannon.) As they were not on bombing missions they had to avoid built-up areas and Luftwaffe controlled airfields where night fighter planes were based.

The only available maps of France that the RAF navigators could study were first-edition ones that had not been updated since the 19th century. Aerial recognition of the landscape had to have the assistance of the moon. Its reflection from ponds, lakes, streams, rivers, canals and railway lines helped orientate the pilots. In remote areas they recognised that the darkest areas were forest and the lighter areas fields. Occasionally, car headlights from a doctor on an emergency mission provided useful illumination as the Germans had introduced the blackout and night curfews.

Pinpointing what was called the 'drop zone' or DZ demanded excellent navigation skills but Charles and his fellow 'boffins', the term used to describe scientific experts, came to their aid. Following the Air Ministry's substantial success developing and employing defensive radar during the Battle of Britain in 1940, the boffins at Telecommunications Research Establishment (TRE) based at Worth Maltravers, near Swanage in Dorset, came up with some new ideas. A small ground-based radar beacon was developed which could emit a signal which could be picked up by receiving equipment on board an airplane. It allowed its operator to determine both the location and the distance of ships and planes. The word 'Radar', an acronym for radio detection and ranging, remained restricted until June 1943, when the Allies

Bedford School's Secret Old Boys

32 Clapham Road, Bedford, where Ethel Bovill lived whilst her sons, Edward and Charles, who attended Bedford School 1918—1925

(Photographed by author, 13th Jan 2010)

released the term to the public.

This top-secret technology was to dramatically improve clandestine night-time air navigation. It was in Beryl Escott's Mission Improbable that she mentions John I. Brown as the designer and world expert of a team which, in the age before transistors, managed to produce a succession of radio equipment for SOE, each an improvement on, and smaller than, the last.

TRE personnel nicknamed the ground portion of this equipment 'Eureka', and the airborne counterpart 'Rebecca'. They began developing test sets for the RAF's Special Duties Squadrons who were flying out on top secret missions. Eureka was to become an invaluable piece of portable electronic equipment carried by agents of the SIS, SOE, the Special Armed Services (SAS) and the American Office of Strategic Services (OSS). It was a compact radar navigation homing beacon named after the Greek expression, "I have found it." Science students will recall that ''Eureka' was shouted out by Archimedes when he understood what happened when he got into the bath. Rebecca is said to have been named after a character in the Old Testament, the wife of Isaac, who was described as crying out for her twins, Esau and Jacob.

Charles's work in Bomber and Coastal Command brought him to the attention of the Special Operations Executive (SOE) and, in October 1941, he was invited to command the radio experimental and flight section of the ISRB. They were very keen on him developing a new radio telephone system.

In the autumn of 1941 I was summoned to an office in Baker St. London where I was interviewed by an Army officer who spoke to me in French. I remarked to him that he had a French Canadian accent and from that moment we got on very well and I was offered the job if I could join them in a month. I was able to arrange this with Marconi's and found myself as a civilian developing the S-phone for the Special

Bedford School's Secret Old Boys

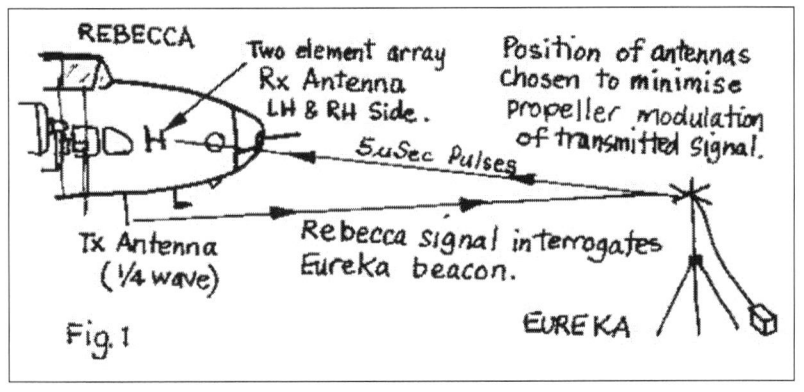

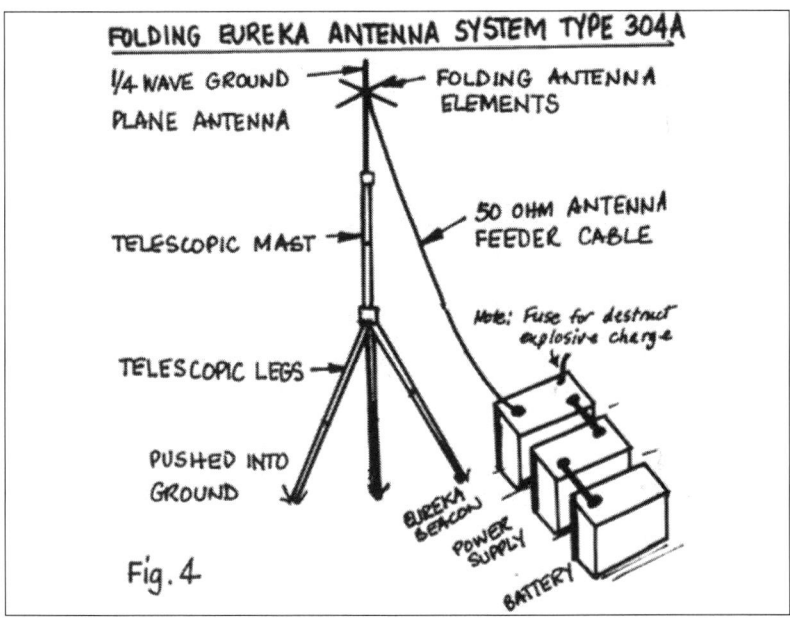

Fig. 1

REBECCA
- Two element array Rx Antenna LH & RH Side.
- Position of antennas chosen to minimise propeller modulation of transmitted signal.
- 5µSec Pulses
- Tx Antenna (¼ wave)
- Rebecca signal interrogates Eureka beacon.
- EUREKA

FOLDING EUREKA ANTENNA SYSTEM TYPE 304A

- ¼ WAVE GROUND PLANE ANTENNA
- FOLDING ANTENNA ELEMENTS
- TELESCOPIC MAST
- 50 OHM ANTENNA FEEDER CABLE
- Note: Fuse for destruct explosive charge
- TELESCOPIC LEGS
- PUSHED INTO GROUND
- EUREKA BEACON
- POWER SUPPLY
- BATTERY

Fig. 4

Top Secret ground-to-air communication system developed by Charles Bovill and other 'boffins' for use by RAF' wireless operators and secret agents 'in the Field'
(http://www.duxfordradiosociety.org/equiphist/reb-eureka/eureka-fig1-598p.jpg)

Operations Executive (SOE). This work, its development and operations is described in an article which I wrote for the British technical journal the 'Electronic world + Wireless World' in September 1993.

Briefly, the S-phone was a duplex UHF radio for use by the resistance for contacting aircraft on parachute drops and for the passing of intelligence to high-flying aircraft. It only had a range of less than a kilometre ground to ground, Thousands of operations took place but it was never detected by the Germans. Flying at 25,000 feet, contact was possible at 50 miles (80km). Soon after joining SOE I was commissioned in the RAF and worked with the Special Duties Squadrons - 138 and 161, which did all of the dropping of supplies to the resistance groups in Europe. (Ibid.)

The 'Ground' transceiver was designed by Captain Bert Lane, and the 'Air' transceiver by Major Hobday, both of the Royal Signals Corps. The S-phone's principal asset was its ability to reduce agents' dread of detection. As it was designed to be able to be carried in a suitcase, the phone enabled SOE-designated aircrew and agents in the field to talk to each other with very little risk of interception. It was also used effectively between motor gunboats landing agents and reception parties on French Mediterranean beaches. In adverse weather conditions like mist, fog and low cloud, a combination of Eureka and the S-phone could help to improve the RAF's accuracy when dropping weapons, supplies and people.

1419 Special Duties Squadron was renamed 419 Squadron and finally 138 Squadron when it was transferred from Newmarket to a newly completed airfield at Tempsford, about eight miles (12km) east of Bedford on 1st March 1942. It had four Wellington Mark III bombers specially modified to trial TR 1335 or 'GEE', another radio navigation system. They were shortly joined by aircrews of the Royal Australian Air Force, the Royal New Zealand Air Force, the Royal Canadian

Bedford School's Secret Old Boys

Eureka Unit

(http://histru.bournemouth.ac.uk/Oral_History/Talking_About_Technology/
radar_research/assets/images/p57-img2.gif 14th December 2009)

Rebecca Unit
(http://www.duxfordradiosociety.org/equiphist/reb-eureka/ind96-100-1.jpg 14th December 2009)

Air Force and, when eventually President Roosevelt joined the Allies, he allocated the 492nd Bombardment Group of the United States Air Force.

Charles joined a very cosmopolitan group of over 2,000 personnel at Tempsford airfield, including Norwegians, French, Poles, Czechoslovakians and South Africans. In order to manage the growing demand from the resistance groups, a second Special Duties Squadron was formed. 161 took responsibility for landing and picking up missions leaving 138 the job of parachuting in agents and supplies.

Charles's value as a specialist aircraft radio engineer was especially appreciated by the Special Duties Squadrons and in April 1942 he was commissioned as a flight lieutenant into the technical, signals and radar branch of the Royal Air Force Volunteer Reserve.

Although not documented, Charles would almost certainly have stayed on base or rented accommodation in nearby Sandy or one of the villages in cycling distance from RAF Tempsford. He would have recognised why some described it as 'the foggiest and boggiest' airfield in the UK and others thought it was disused. Most of the buildings for the technical staff, engineering, administration, canteen, officers' and sergeants' mess and living quarters were brick-built but contained a mixture of steel and asbestos. Some were clad in wood and it was said that they were built to resemble animal sheds.

This was Jasper Maskelyne's work. He was an illusionist, famous for his magic shows in London before the war. Surprisingly, these skills were in great demand during wartime. He was appointed a Major and his 'Magic gang' based at the Royal Engineers' Camouflage Experimental Station adapted his conjuring and illusionist expertise to the battlefield on a large scale. His magic was also put into practice at Tempsford. The construction of the site involved the knocking down of several cottages and farm buildings. Port Mahon Farm was occupied by pilots who were taught the vital skill of recognising the silhouettes of planes. The roof

Bedford School's Secret Old Boys

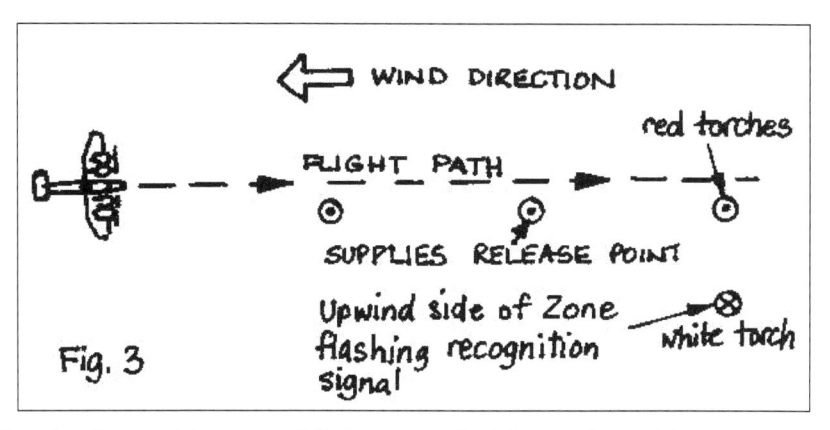

Fig. 3 — WIND DIRECTION / FLIGHT PATH / SUPPLIES RELEASE POINT / red torches / Upwind side of Zone flashing recognition signal / white torch

The L-shaped layout of lights needed for a drop. The reception committee would place the Eureka unit nearby and light the torches when they heard the aircraft approaching. The S-Phone allowed vital messages to be sent to the radio operator on the plane who would then send them to SOE, SIS, SAS or OSS HQ when the plane returned to RAF Tempsford.
(http://www.duxfordradiosociety.org/equiphist/reb-eureka/eureka-fig3-601p.jpg 14th December 2009)

Training to use the S-Phone. Ten-day intensive courses were run for reception committee personnel at Howbury Hall, Renhold, Bedford, only five miles (8km) from RAF Tempsford..
(www.cvni.net/radio/e2k/e2k035/e2k35cs.html 19th December 2009)

slates of Gibraltar Farm were removed to make it look derelict. Windows had the glass deliberately broken. Sacks were draped across the inside of the windows instead of curtains. Some doors were left hanging from only one hinge. For the same reason much of the black Bedfordshire weather-boarding was removed. The adjacent farm buildings got the same treatment.

Inside Gibraltar Farm it was said that the stairs, ceiling and first floor were removed to create a very large room. The inside walls were built up and reinforced. This was to become the airfield's nerve centre. All the hangars and domestic buildings were camouflaged to blend in with the surrounding farmland and it is said that they were all thatched – to give the impression that they were farm buildings. Visitors reported seeing them mildewed, cobwebbed and covered in mould.

Nissen huts resembled pig sties. Outside Gibraltar Farm the pond was left with the odd few ducks. Rusty old tractors were left outside but moved occasionally in the fields and yards. Large grey and green markings and several metres wide black lines were painted on the concrete runways to give the overflying Luftwaffe pilots the impression that they were patches of grass or the continuation of the hedge. Cattle were deliberately grazed on some of the fields when the runways were not in use so that the land might be thought to be being used for agricultural purposes. It succeeded. It is said that the aerial photographs taken by German air crew who flew over the airfield were interpreted as it being disused.

Another secret establishment in Bedfordshire Charles would very likely have visited was Howbury Hall, an 18th century country house set in a large estate near Renhold, about three miles (4.8km) east of Bedford and five miles (8km) west of Tempsford.

In David Hewson's introduction to the reprinted Moondrop to Gascony, an account of Anne-Marie Walter's wartime experiences as an SOE courier who was flown out of RAF

Bedford School's Secret Old Boys

Using the S-Phone in daylight. It was normally used at night.
http://www.pathfindergroupuk.com/2005/p_ruvien%20au%20S-Phone.jpg 14th December 2009

Gibraltar Farm, RAF Tempsford, Bedfordshire, nerve centre of operations on a n airfield designed by an illusionist to look disused. Hitler was said to be aware of this' viper's nest' but it was never attacked throughout the war.
(Courtesy of John Button)

Tempsford, he suggests Howbury Hall, named by the SOE as Special Training School 40, was opened in early 1943 following serious mistakes by agents handling the S-Phone and the ground-to-air communications system.

According to Stephen Bunker in his *Spy Capital of Britain*, it was under the command of a Major Tidmarsh who had a team of five officers and thirty-seven personnel of other ranks. Whilst it remains undocumented whether Charles worked there, it seems very likely. A ten-day training courses in using the most up-to-date models of Rebecca, Eureka and the S-phone was provided. Those men and women destined to work with the reception committees in Norway, Poland, Czechoslovakia, Denmark, Holland, Belgium, France, Italy, Greece and Yugoslavia needed first-hand experience of using it before they were flown out from Tempsford.

By December 1944, practically all the Special Duty planes had been fitted with 'Rebecca' and, because of the top secret nature of the work it was being used for, its range and frequencies remained classified until the end of the war. Jim Peake, a navigator with 138 Squadron, described Rebecca in his memoirs as a radio beacon consisting of a black box with a retractable 11 foot (3.3 m) aerial. They were lowered out from the back of the plane and had to be wound back in before landing. Some planes had two bi-pole aerials attached either side of the fuselage. The battery-operated, light-weight Eureka transmitters, able to be strapped to someone's chest, were dropped in carefully padded panniers to the waiting reception committee and hidden in hedges or under straw close to the DZ. The ground operator could preset the intensity of the 'blips' to create a radio beam down which the pilot of the aircraft could fly.

The beauty of the Eureka, Peake said, was that it used very little power and could be used to guide an aircraft to a dropping ground without the use of lights or flares, no matter how dark the night. It was only switched on when the approaching aircraft had its Rebecca switched on. Provided that it was sited in a suitable location, pilots could easily

Bedford School's Secret Old Boys

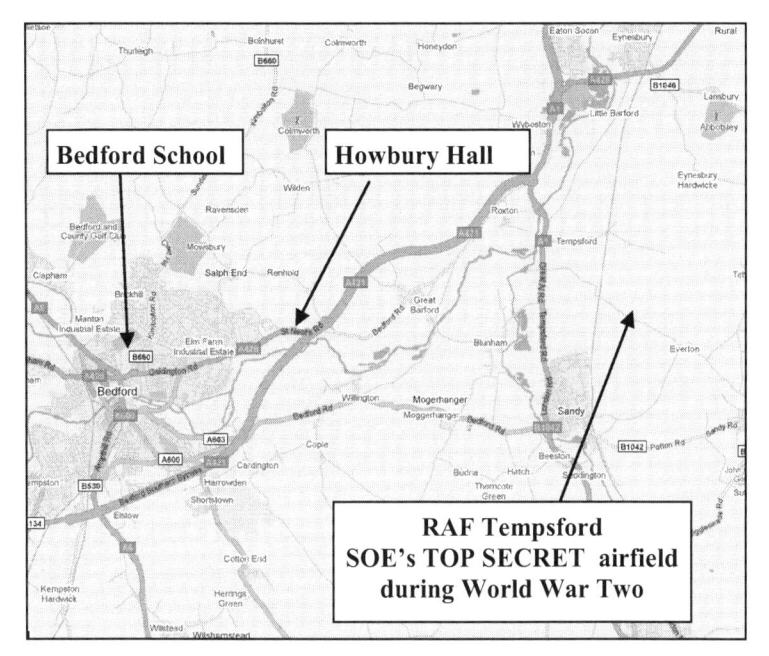

[Map showing Bedford School, Howbury Hall, and RAF Tempsford – SOE's TOP SECRET airfield during World War Two]

Google map extract showing places in Bedfordshire important in Charles Bovill's life.

Photography of **Howbury Hall**, near Renhold, east of Bedford. During World War Two it was requisitioned and agents were trained in the latest Eureka and S-phone equipment before being flown out of RAF Tempsford.

(Bernard O'Connor)

guide the aircraft to within 100 yards (91 m) of the box. They had a range of at least 30 miles (48km) at 2,000 feet so navigators did not need recourse to GEE or map reading. Wing Commander Leonard Ratcliff of 161 Squadron reported in his memoirs that he got a Rebecca signal 38 miles from one of his targets. Thanks to Charles and his fellow boffins, there were claims it could be picked up to 60 miles (96 kms.) away.

When the ground-based radio operator learned that the enemy were in the area, they had to move their Eureka sets elsewhere. Sometimes they or a brave resistance member hid them in bundles of firewood tied to theirs backs or the cross bar of a bicycle and tried to avoid an over-curious guard at a check point.

Some of the early Eureka sets were captured in Holland, Belgium and France and were successfully used to guide RAF Tempsford pilots to German-controlled DZs where the containers were dropped. The gunners on the flak batteries were told not to shoot them down until they were on their way back. Captured agents, under torture, had agreed to play back their radio sets to London in what became known as the 'Englandspiel'. Many agents were arrested on landing and hundreds of resistance group members were identified, arrested, imprisoned, tortured and executed. Thousands of tons of weapons, ammunition, clothes, food, medical supplies and money fell directly into enemy hands.

Consequently, when the double-cross eventually became known in SOE HQ in mid-1943, instructions went out requesting that subsequent Eureka models had to include a self-destruct detonator to avoid them falling into enemy hands.

Brave French steeplejacks positioned two Eurekas, nick-named 'Boot' and 'Shoe', on the pinnacles of Rheims and Orleans cathedrals. This was a great navigational help, as the pilot did not have to fly close to these heavily defended cities. By the end of 1943, Eureka beacons had been planted in three of the great French forests. To help with Operation

Bedford School's Secret Old Boys

One of 138 Squadron's Stirling bombers modified to carry agents and supplies and equipped with Rebecca to allow radio communication with the reception committee.
(Courtesy of Bill Bright)

Westland Lysander used to take and pick up agents and VIPs from RAF Tempsford (and RAF Tangmere on south coast). Note the ladder to allow quicker access for the agents.
(www.jaapteeuwen.com/.../westland%20lysander.jpg 18th December 2009)

Bedford School's Secret Old Boys

Market Garden, the Allied invasion of Holland, sets were placed in the Ardennes, wooded hills in eastern Belgium.

Although they were unmanned, a local reception committee was sent in to pick up any containers that were dropped on these 'targets' should the pilot not have been able to spot the correct recognition letter that had to be flashed in Morse code from a hand-held torch on the ground at the designated DZ.

Peake told of how 138 and 161 Squadron planes were fitted with a 6-inch (15 cm) circular screen with a trace line down the centre. A green pulse line projected either side of this line depending on the location of Rebecca. There was a vertical scale between 0 – 90 miles (0 - 144 km) and a switch converted it to 0 – 9 miles (0 - 14 km). By turning a few degrees to port or starboard, the pilot could easily home in. In fact, he wrote, it made the return flight to Tempsford "a piece of cake" for an "idle or tired out Nav."

Michael Foot, the SOE historian, reported that pocket radios were designed to avoid the shortcomings of the rather bulky Eureka and S-Phones. While SIS developed the 'paraset', which weighed 1.6 kg, a group of Poles working in a factory at Letchworth, produced transceivers that made other Allied equipment look like museum pieces. They were reluctant to let any be handed over to other sections of SOE. Sets, said to cost £12,000 to manufacture in 1944, were issued to agents going into Germany from which they could communicate with radio operators on overflying planes at pre-determined times. (O'Connor, B. *RAF Tempsford: Bedfordshire's TOP SECRET Airfield during World War Two*, private publication)

Whether Charles revisited his old school during the time he spent in Bedfordshire is unknown. The students would undoubtedly have been enthralled by an account of the work he was involved with but, having signed the Official Secrets Act, he was not at liberty to tell anyone what he was doing.

After regularly accompanying special duties' aircrew to install, test and also to operate S-phone and other equipment

Bedford School's Secret Old Boys

Lockheed Hudson used to land and pick up agents and VIPs in occupied Europe.
(www.2iemeguerre.com/avions/images/image1468.jpg 18th December 2009)

Modified Halifax Bomber used by Special Duties Squadrons (lost over Czechoslovakia on 15th March 1943).
(www.harringtonmuseum.org.uk/138%20Halifax.jpg 18th December 2009)

over France, Charles was posted in June 1944 to SOE's Force 399 in Italy. His prime task was to equip aircraft of the Balkan Air Force with the S-phone and Eureka, thus enhancing the Allies' communication with Josip Broz (Tito) and his communist partisans in Yugoslavia, to whom the RAF were dropping a variety of equipment and liaison officers. The Balkan Air Force also helped the resistance groups in Albania, Greece and Poland. However, his time in Italy was cut short.

> *I returned to England, as a result of the injuries in Italy and then operated the same kind of activity in Holland but we used* (de Havilland) *Mosquitoes for long range penetrations over Germany and for short ranges used the smallest aircraft, the Auster.* (http://securityriskmanagement.eu/content1.asp?cID=charlesbovill-en 12th December 2009)

In a tribute to Charles's work with the Euro-American Technical Centre for Security Training, it was claimed that he was a close friend of Major Anthony Deane-Hammond. An Internet search revealed that he was Second-in-Command of the 1st Airborne Divisional Signals, one of the British groups involved in Operation Market Garden. This was the planned invasion of Holland in September 1944 which got stopped at what became known as 'The Bridge too Far' over the Lower Rhine at Arnhem. Charles's technical skills in radio equipment were also needed in land transport. On a page on the Major's wartime exploits on the Pegasusarchive website it states that,

> *...they were immediately concerned about the distance from the drop zones to the bridge, as they knew that the limited range of their radio sets would result in a blackout between the two areas until on the second day, when the Division was able to advance on Arnhem. To overcome this problem, Deane-*

Bedford School's Secret Old Boys

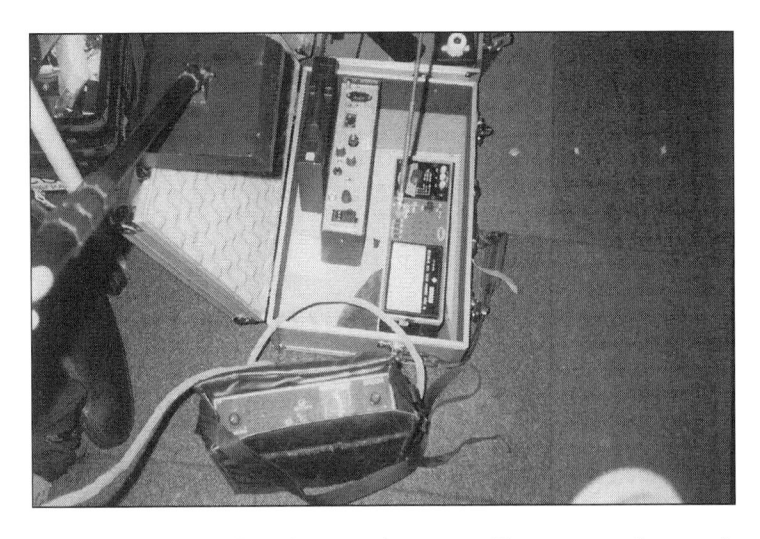

Charles's 'Broom' - electronic surveillance equipment
(Courtesy of Klas Nilsson)

ANTI-SURVEILLANCE ELECTRONIC EQUIPMENT

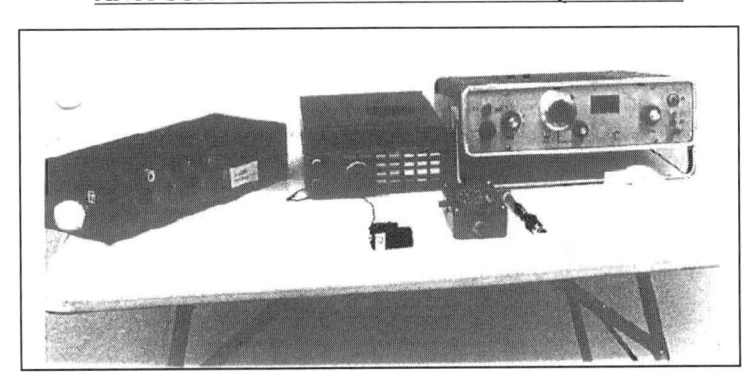

LOW FREQUENCY RECEIVER 10KHz TO 600 KHz FM, AM Sens: 2uV	TYPE 9600 RECEIVER 60 to 960 MHz FM,AM,SSB Subcarrier	BDRECEIVER 20 MHz to 1GHz FM, AM and Subcarrier BDRec Charger

Extract from an Electronic Surveillance Brochure
(Courtesy of Klas Nilsson)

Drummond would have liked to have taken more of the powerful Jeep-mounted Type 19 sets that, at present, only the gunners of the 1st Airlanding Light Regiment used. However to take more of these would require additional gliders, of which there were none, and the planning phase for Market Garden was so short that there was no time to work a way around this problem, so Divisional Signals therefore had to make do with what they had. Deane-Drummond noted after Arnhem that absolutely everyone was so keen to get into battle, after so many previous cancellations, that many such risks were knowingly taken.

Upon arriving in Arnhem, Deane-Drummond was pleased to discover that their radio sets appeared to be working perfectly, but as the 1st Parachute Brigade moved closer towards Arnhem the clarity of their signals began to deteriorate rapidly. Although the Brigade was only two or three miles away at this stage, the medium-range jeep-mounted Type 22 sets were not able to make contact with them at all. Major Deane-Drummond ordered one of these sets to be driven forward, half way between Divisional Headquarters and the 1st Parachute Brigade, in the hope that messages could be relayed back and forth, however the signal from this jeep quickly faded away.

On Monday 18th September, to inform them of a new radio frequency for the day, Deane-Drummond left Divisional HQ and set out to where the remains of the 1st Parachute Brigade were continuing their efforts to break through to the Bridge. (http:// www.pegasusarchive. org/arnhem/ deane_drummond.htm 13th December 2009)

When the Allies eventually invaded Germany in Spring 1945, Charles was reported by the Euro-American Technical Centre for Security Training website as being on board a plane over Berlin when he used his radio equipment to pick

Bedford School's Secret Old Boys

CHARLES B BOVILL

C.Eng_, M.I.E.E., F.I.E.R.E., M.R_Ae.S.

V AT No. 2129068 74
NON-LINEAR JUNCTION DETECTOR

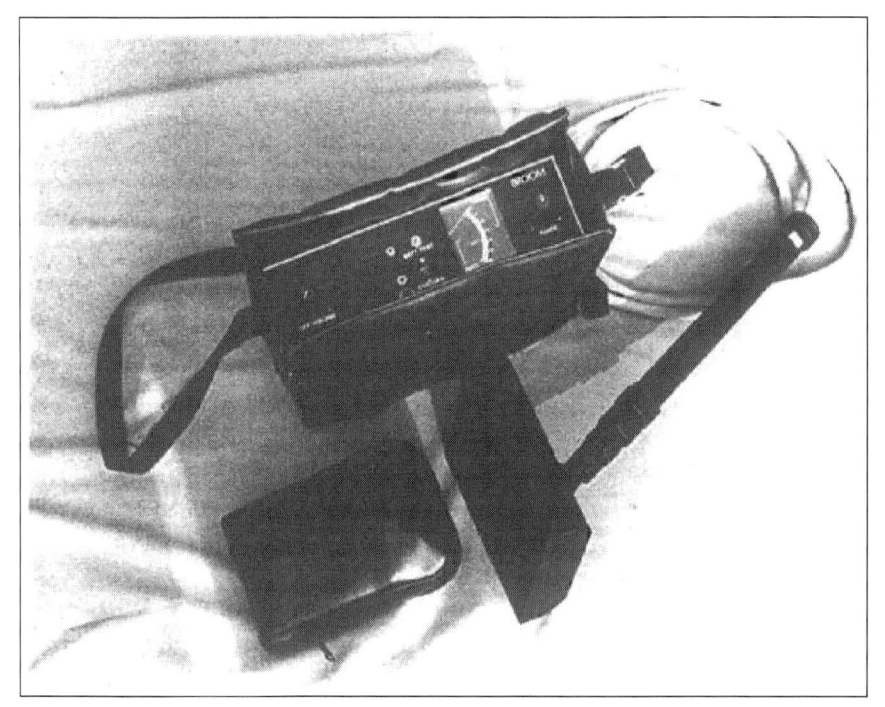

The instrument consists of two basic items:

1. The detector unit which is slung over the shoulder when operating
2. The Search Antenna. This has a telescopic handle extending to five feet.
It is used to sweep over the luggage being checked.

Indication of the presence of any item, whether switched on or off, is given by an audible like sound.

(Extract from an Electronic Surveillance Brochure courtesy of Klas Nilsson) the conversations of Wehrmacht staff, the German military. Whether it had any significance in the final outcome of the war was not mentioned.

The same website refers to his friendship with Captain Sir Basil Liddel-Hart (1895 – 1970), the Daily Telegraph's military correspondent in 1925-32 and military adviser to The Times in 1935-9. During the war he wrote for the Daily Mail and afterwards became a writer of military history. Exactly what link there was between him and Charles is not known; it was probably in the field of Military Intelligence.

> On the day the war finished, which none of us realised was going to occur. I was sent for by the Commanding Officer of the SOE station and he said, "You are out of the action tomorrow. I have a signal from London to say that they have an arrangement with Marconi's that you will return to them on the day upon which the European War ceases."
>
> I flew home next day and two days later I was back at my desk at Marconi's. It was really too much of an anti-climax after all of the excitement. I could not settle down after all the activity. I felt that things were too slow, much as I liked Marconi's. I was sent to take a Frenchman round the British Industry to show our latest developments and amongst the firms visited, was Decca Navigator which Company had just perfected a brilliant new hyperbolic navigation system. I immediately got on very well with Ted Lewis, the chairman, and with Harvey Schwarz, the technical director. He said to me, "Come and run the Air Development side of the Navigator Company. I do not know what you are earning but I will double it if you can start here in a month."
>
> At 34 you do not turn down such offers and I was doing their experiments in the air 5 weeks later. I had 14 wonderful years under Sir Edward Lewis, working all over Europe, France with experiments with their Air Force, Air France, Alitalia, Danish Airlines, American

Bedford School's Secret Old Boys

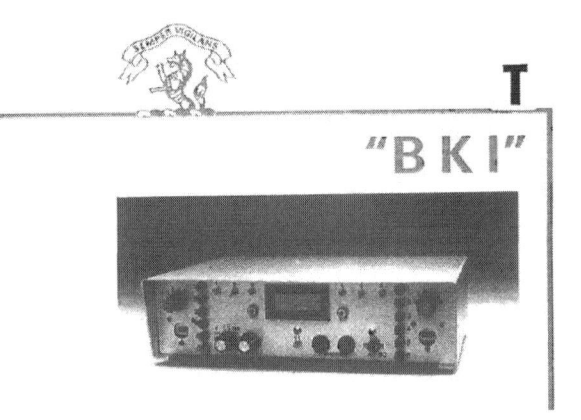

"B K I"

TELEPHONE
CHECKING
EQUIPMENT

BKI is an easy to use unit designed for the rapid testing of telephone instruments and lines. It is small in size and weighs only 6lbs.
The design is based upon the break-in method, and overcomes many of the problems in testing modern electronic communications.
BKI eliminates the need for making connections to any parts of the telephone system except between the new wall type sockets and the instrument.
A built-in digital volt-ammeter checks on-and-off hook conditions. There are outputs to a headset and tape recorder. Accessories are provided for connection to all known terminals.
A comprehensive switching system enables tests to be made for unauthorised attachments, line taps and phantom circuits.
The BKI has a rechargeable self-contained battery which will operate for 30 hours between charges. When used in conjunction with Larsen, Broom and SR7, the BKI completes the range of equipment needed for total counter-surveillance operations.

The equipment can be used on 1 wire or 6 wire systems. The digital volt ammeter can be isolated from the internal circuits enabling it to be used as an independent instrument.
SENSITIVITY: For functions of volt ammeter a 50mV output to headset.
POWER CONSUMPTION (Battery operated) at full audio output 50mA
CHARGER: AC power consumption 10Q. Charger input voltage 115/210V (1060Hz) Fused
CONTROLS: On/Off with LED. 2 six position rotary switches, 6 toggle switches for cross line testing. 5 position meter switch: 0 20V. 0 200V, 0 20mA 0 200mA, AUDIOGAIN (Variable)
INPUTS/OUTPUTS: Socket for external use of volt ammeter. When used in this mode a switch isolates the meter. 2 input sockets, 2 telephone jacks, Charger socket with Charging LED.
FINISH: Brushed aluminium case. Switches and input sockets colour coded.
DIMENSIONS: 300 x 76 x 211 mm, 12" x 3" x 8". Weight 2.7kg, 6lbs.
ACCESSORIES: Instructions, Set of adaptor cables, Headset, Attache carrying case.

SECURITY RESEARCH AND DEVELOPMENT LTD

Bedford School's Secret Old Boys

Airlines. Experiments were carried out in over 100 different types of aircraft. Then everything changed, I met a very beautiful lady (Mrs Pamela Keegan (nee Bryan), *and we got married.* (Ibid.)

According to his obituary in the *Daily Telegraph*, Charles enjoyed a fulfilling career with Decca, the London-based gramophone manufacturer, where he was much involved with the creation, development and sales of the company's internationally successful Decca Navigator marine equipment.

During his time with Decca, the prnewswire website, reported that the name

...Decca became a piece of nautical terminology that epitomised security and dependability. At its peak there were chains in all of the principal shipping areas of the world and an estimated 200,000 Decca users in Europe alone. By measuring the differences in signals received from transmitters along many of the world's coastlines, mariners and aviators were able to establish their positions with a degree of accuracy and consistency previously considered impossible. The advent of GPS navigation satellites eventually made the service superfluous and the General Lighthouse Authority, which had been funding Racal to maintain and operate the Decca chains, finally ended its support on 31st March 2000. (http://www.prnewswire.co.uk/cgi/news/release? id=19360 4th February 2010)

For understandable reasons, Charles's involvement with Military Intelligence was not mentioned in his obituary. However, a translation of the Euro-American Technical Centre for Security Training website states that,

Bedford School's Secret Old Boys

Following the War, Charles Bovill passes depend on reorganization of DI-6 (Department Intelligence-6), real name of the Foreign Intelligence known as MI-6 or S.I.S. (Special Intelligence Service) to develop an incredible technical work on the adaptation and creation Systems, working with the Intelligence Electronic GCHQ UK or in compliance his deep commitment, starting to internal conferences and teaching experience to the American Electronic Intelligence (NSA) to Agents S.D.E.C.E.(Intelligence Defense) or the German MAD (Military Intelligence), in Interception methodologies. (http://www.eatcst-itd-inc.com/miembros.htm, 4th February 2010)

In the early 1970s he changed jobs yet again. In his interview with Security Risk Management he admitted that

I had been abroad more than 1,000 times and thought that now I wanted to be at home. I left Decca and got a job in London developing Cable TV systems but, whilst I was still young enough, I must get down to developing devices and systems. I was attracted to technical security as at the time there was a lot of development to do in this field and I have now been in this work for over 20 years. I have a laboratory in the garden of my home and get great satisfaction from the development work which I do and the ECS and Sweeps which I frequently carry out. (http://securityriskmanagement.eu/content1.asp?cID=charlesbovill-en 12th December 2009)

In 1972 he joined Allen International as their technical director. Soon the showcases at the company's Westminster premises were displaying sophisticated security equipment which was similar to that developed by SOE's boffins in their workshops at the Thatched Barn, a requisitioned hotel on the A1 Barnet by-pass.

Bedford School's Secret Old Boys

During the war they had manufactured "Giglis", a very flexible surgical saw of interlaced cutting wire, which could be concealed in a cap badge, an ordinary boot or shoelace. They were vital for captured secret agents to help them escape from prison cells which had metal bars across the windows. Some bicycle pumps had torches specially built into the handle end. Compasses were hidden in specially-made fountain pens, shaving brushes, hairbrushes, pipes, golf balls and dominoes. Miniature batteries and miniature cameras were sent. Tiny telescopes, one and a half inches long by half an inch wide (39 x 13 mm), were made to look like cigarette lighters! These were some of the 'Q gadgets' provided by the appropriately called Clothing Department of the Ministry of Supply headed by Charles Fraser-Smith. The 'Q War' is the focus of his book The Secret War of Charles Fraser-Smith.

Much of the SOE's lethal scientific research and development took place at Station IX, a former hotel called 'The Frythe' near Welwyn, Hertfordshire. It is now a research centre for pharmaceutical giant SmithKline Beecham. As well as delayed action fuses and incendiaries, the boffins developed a silent pistol for assassination jobs, a tear gas gun designed as a pen and cigarettes that blew up when lit. Particularly fascinating were their anti-personnel explosive devices concealed in cavities inside actual everyday objects or in life-size replicas made of plaster or celluloid. These included exploding rusty nuts and bolts, wooden clogs, Chianti wine bottles, screw-top milk bottles, fountain pens, railway fishplates (joint bars), oilcans, life belts, bicycle pumps, food tins, soap, shaving brushes, books, loaves of bread, lumps of coal, rock, turnips, beetroots, stuffed mice and rats and horse, cow and camel dung! Even lethal toilet paper was made.

Agents' wireless transmitting sets were hidden in hollowed-out logs, granite blocks, concrete rubble, faggots (bundles of wood), artists' paint boxes, portable gramophones, office equipment such as adding machines, record players and even bathroom scales, paint and oil drums, car batteries, furniture such as armchairs, cement sacks, vacuum cleaners, driftwood, workmen's tool boxes, electrical testing meters, massage sets and continental wireless sets. Since wireless operators often hid their sets in lavatory cisterns, a lavatory chain was devised, which acted as an aerial. Miniature communication receivers were hidden in clocks, other household goods as well as in hard-backed German Bibles. Few things were sacred in war.

Charles had clearly learned from these devices as his display included microphones disguised as wrist watches and cufflinks, and microphones and radio transmitters attached surreptitiously to ties, fountain pens and table lighters. As the Chief of SOE's Technical Branch and later General Service Branch MI6, Charles was known affectionately by the International Bodyguard Association as 'Q'. This was the name Ian Fleming gave the quartermaster of the new-fangled technology in the James Bond books. In fact,

The business provided Q-type gadgets for James Bond films while also building a reputation in the Middle East and elsewhere for security, espionage and counter-espionage equipment. One of Bovill's most effective designs was a crowd-control device which used a photic drive. (www.64-baker-street.org/*obituaries/* obit_2001_charles_bovill.html 4th February 2009)

With the bomb attacks by the IRA (Irish Republican Army) in London and Birmingham and large anti-government demonstrations during the 1970s and 80s, Charles's equipment was used by the British Police Force. Manchester City Council's Police Monitoring Unit reported that his photic drive was a 10-30 Hz strobe light which produced seizures, giddiness, nausea, and fainting. Adding sound pulses in the 4.0 - 7.5 Hz range increased its effectiveness and it was used in the 'Valkyrie', advertised in the British Defence

Equipment Catalogue until 1983 as a "frequency" weapon. In Kim Besley's Electropollution, he described the squawk box or sound curdler as using two loudspeakers of 350 watt output to emit two slightly different frequencies which combine in the ear to produce a shrill shrieking noise.

After trying out the device on his wife, Pamela, in his laboratory at West Byfleet, Charles marketed his invention in America, where prison authorities were impressed by its ability to control disruptive inmates and riots. This was despite the U.S. National Science Foundation report which stated that it had a "*severe risk of permanent impairment of hearing.*"

On October 1st, 1973, the staff at Allen International was monitoring one of the firm's spy camera products when they observed a suspicious-looking figure lurking at the entrance. When they confronted the man, he threw a bomb inside the doorway and ran away. The device did not explode but was found to contain five pounds (2.2 kg) of gelignite. Police reports hinted that it had been an IRA attack.

In Klas Nilsson's introduction to the interview he had with Charles, he mentioned that, amongst other things, he had invented the 'Larsen' and the 'Broom'. A clue as to what this equipment was for was the comment that, "*His inventions make the job a lot easier for the professionals within the Electronic Counter Surveillance business.*" An Internet search found Larsen and Broom mentioned in Baron James Shortt of Castleshort's instructional advice to the International Bodyguard Association.

> *The next phase of electronic search is location. This is first done with a piece of equipment called a Larsen which relies on acoustic feedback. Acoustic feedback is what occurs when you take a transmitting microphone too close to a speaker and it starts to howl. However, if the transmitter is not functioning at the time, a Larsen will not detect it. This may be because the device has been remotely switched off (a favourite with the FBI) or because the opposition has bought cheap Chinese*

batteries and they have drained down (favourite with ... well, let's just say they're British!)
If the transmitter isn't transmitting, you need a device called the Broom or Non Linear Junction Detector (NLJD). The Broom was developed by the IBA's ECS instructor Charles Bovill. It detects electronic components whether or not they are transmitting at the time. The drawback is that it will also detect TV sets, electronic alarm clocks, microwave ovens and anything else that contains electronic components. The Broom must be used in conjunction with the Larsen. Both these items can be used against telephone devices. (http://www.iba-deutschland.de/files/iba-baron-castleshorts-instructional-notes.pdf 18th December 2009)

To have left Bedford School at fourteen, gone on to university and become so knowledgeable about ground-to-air radio equipment that he was sent to work with the top secret Special Duties Squadrons during the Second World War is no mean achievement. To have been recognised by military intelligence as a man who could be relied upon to help with specialised electronic equipment and then be headhunted to work around the world with various defence agencies indicates a particularly talented man. To have been compared with 'Q', the character in the James Bond books and have been involved in international electronic counter surveillance technology means that Charles Bovill deserves to be a role model for many a Bedford schoolboy.

This 'Old Bedfordian' continued to experiment and invent in his home laboratory in West Byfleet until shortly before his death in 2001. On his letterhead he stated that he was a Chartered Engineer, a member of the Institute of Electrical Engineers, Fellow of the Institute of Electronic and Radio Engineers and a Member of the Royal Aeronautical Society.

Conclusion

These Bedford School Old Boys made significant contributions to the Allied cause during World War Two. Given the secret nature of their work, very few people were aware of what they had done. Signing the Official Secrets Act probably meant that in many cases, they were not able to tell their family and friends exactly what they did during the war. This book is a tribute to their bravery and ingenuity, an attempt to give them a more public recognition.

One imagines that present and future Old Boys will similarly volunteer to engage in secret operations, should they ever be approached by Britain's intelligence services.

Bibliography

Atkinson, R. (2002), *An Army at Dawn*, Holt Paperbacks, New York,
Bunker, S. (2007), *The Spy Capital of Britain: Bedfordshire's secret war 1939-1945*, Bedford Chronicles
Burton, C. (2005), *Air Power History*, Winter,
Clark, F. (1999), *Agents by Moonlight*, Tempus Publishing
Crawley, A. 'The Limpet Mine & 171-175 Tavistock Street', *BAALHS*, (April 2012)
Darling, D. (1975), *Secret Sunday*, Kimber, London,
Darling, D. (1977), *Sunday at Large*, Kimber, London,
Foot, M.R.D. (1999), *SOE: The Special Operations Executive 1940 – 1946*, Pimlico
Jeffrey, Keith (2010), *MI6 - The History of the Secret Intelligence Service 1909-1949*, Bloomsbury
Johns, P. (1979), *Within Two Cloaks: Missions with SIS and SOE*, William Kimber
London Gazette, 18 May 1943
Macrae, S. (1971), *Winston Churchill's Toyshop*, Kineton, The Roundwood Press
MacKenzie, S. (2002), *The Secret History of S.O.E.: Special Operations Executive 1940-1945*, St Ermin's Press
McBride, S. (2012), *The Bravest Canadian*, Granville Island Publishing
McDonnell, P.K. (2004), *Operatives, Spies and Saboteurs*, Citadel Press,
Montgomery-Massingberd, H. (1976), *Burke's Irish Family Records*. London, U.K.: Burkes Peerage Ltd,
O'Connor, B. (2010), *RAF Tempsford: Churchill's MOST SECRET Airfield*, Amberley
Philby, K. (2003), *My Secret War: The Autobiography of a Spy*, Arrow Books,
Smith, C.F., Lesberg, S. & McKnight, G. (1981), *The Secret War of Charles Fraser-Smith,* Michael Joseph, London
Stafford, D. (1980), *Britain and European Resistance 1940-1945*, Macmillan Oxford

Sweet-Escott, B. (1965), *Baker Street Irregular*. Methuen, London
The Daily Telegraph, Charles Bovill's Obituary, 9 May 2001
The Times, Frank Nelson's Obituary 13 August, 1966
Turner, D. (2006), *Station XII Aston House SOE's Secret Centre*, Sutton
Walters, A. (2009), *Moondrop to Gascony*, Moho Books, Wiltshire
West, N. (1984), *M16: British Secret Intelligence Service Operations 1909 – 1945*, Random House,
Wildman, R. and Crawley, A. (2003), *Bedford's Motoring Heritage*, Sutton Publishing

Websites
http://www.2iemeguerre.com/avions/images/image1468.jpg 18th December 2009
http://www.64-baker-street.org/obituaries/obit_2001_charles_bovill.html 4th February 209
http://www.bandhpast.co.uk/barcombe/b0428build.php 11th January 2010
http://www.cvni.net/radio/e2k/e2k035/e2k35cs.html 19th December 2009
http://www.duxfordradiosociety.org/equiphist/reb-eureka/eureka-fig1-598p.jpg 14th December 2009
http://www.duxfordradiosociety.org/equiphist/reb-eureka/eureka-fig4-640p.jpg 14th December 2009
http://www.duxfordradiosociety.org/equiphist/reb-eureka/eureka-fig3-601p.jpg 14th December 2009
http://www.duxfordradiosociety.org/equiphist/reb-eureka/ind96-100-1.jpg 14th December 2009
http://www.duxfordradiosociety.org/restoration/restoredequip/tr3174/tr3174.html
http://www.eatcst-itd-inc.com/miembros.htm 4th February 2010
http://www.gommecourt.co.uk/.../QWR/Bovill%20QWR1.jpg 11th January 2010
http://www.harringtonmuseum.org.uk/138%20Halifax.jpg 18th

December 2009
http://www.historyofpa.co.uk/gfx/cw/2lo/girl.jpg 4th February 2010
http://histru.bournemouth.ac.uk/Oral_History/
Talking_About_Technology/radar_research/assets/images/p57-img2.gif 14th December 2009
http://www.iba-deutschland.de/files/iba-baron-castleshorts-instructional-notes.pdf 18th December 2009
http://www.jaapteeuwen.com/.../westland%20lysander.jpg 18th December 2009
http://www.nwbotanicals.org/oak/newphysics/synthtele/synthtele.html 18th December 2009
http://www.pathfindergroupuk.com/2005/p_ruvien%20au%20S-Phone.jpg 14th December 2009
http://www.pegasusarchive.org/arnhem/deane_drummond.htm 13th December 2009
http://www.r-type.org/static/crystal.htm 10th January 2010
http://www.securitymanager.se/images/Charles_Bovill.jpg 18th December 2009
http://securityriskmanagement.eu/content1.asp?cID=charlesbovill-en 18th December 2009
http://www.telegraph.co.uk/news/obituaries/1329575/Charles-Bovill.html
http://www.wired.com/.../2008/09/radio_1921_630px.jpg 10th January 2010
http://www.bbc.co.uk/ww2peopleswar/stories/97/a4372797.shtml
http://www.bbc.co.uk/ww2peopleswar/stories/52/a5961152.shtml
http://www.bbc.co.uk/ww2peopleswar/stories/34/a5961134.shtml
http://www.combinedops.com/Cockleshell%20Heroes.htm
http://www.realmilitaryflix.com/public/253.cfm
http://www.realmilitaryflix.com/public/203.cfm?sd=61
http://www.elgrancapitan.org/foro/search.php?t=18627&sid=359e0dc2e3e9f472d39b806a0d50a49
www.rafinfo.org.uk/rafescape/guerisse.htm

Bedford School's Secret Old Boys

www.conscript-heroes.com/Pat%20Line%20page.html
http://www.psicothema.com/psicothema.asp?id=67
http://www.navalandmilitarymuseum.org/resource_pages/heroes/peters.html
http://thebravestcanadian.wordpress.com/category/frederic-thornton-peters/
http://www.navalandmilitarymuseum.org/resource_pages/heroes/peters.html
http://thebravestcanadian.wordpress.com/category/royal-navy/
http://www.navalandmilitarymuseum.org/images/peters11.gif
http://www.jhplc.com/images/body-jhcl-01.jpg
http://discoveringbristol.org.uk/images/sized/images/uploads/slavery/Photograph12-400x303.jpg
http://www.specialforcesroh.com/roll-4066.html
http://www.cqbservices.com/?page_id=61/
http://en.wikipedia.org/wiki/Frank_Nelson_(politician)
http://home.earthlink.net/~mrstephenson_umsl/spy2/organization.html
http://www.cqbservices.com/?page_id=61/
(http://www.oxforddnb.com/view/article/35198)
http://www.stroud-history.org.uk/articles.php?article_id=11
http://www.sfclub.org/history.htm
http://intelligenceref.blogspot.com/2010/11/z-organisation.html

Publications

Email communication with Niall Creed, 28th June, 2011; 18th August 2011

Documents in the National Archives
HS9 372/1, David Maitland Makgill Crighton
HS9 321/8 Cecil Vandepeer Clarke
HS9 36/6 Mike Andrews

Bedford School's Secret Old Boys